# *The Secret Book of Free Money*

Introduction

   Thank you for your purchase. This guide was put together to help those trying to help themselves through hard work and determination. Whether you are starting or expanding a business, looking to start a community based project, or any number of ideas or projects, nothing can be accomplished without the proper funding. There is a grant or loan program to help almost everyone.

   This book is sold with the understanding that the author and publisher are not giving legal or professional advice in any way. There are no guarantees either expressed or implied for the information given within.  The information contained in this guide is believed to be reliable and up to date at the time of publication however, like anything else, programs change from time to time and there is no guarantee that the continuance of any program is implied.

   The authors are not agents for any programs listed within.  This book is sold for information purposes only and is not intended to be a replacement for proper professional advice and recommendations. Neither the author nor publisher will be held liable for any transactions with any person, proprietorship, partnership, company, corporation or association listed in this guide.

   The best way to use this guide is determine what your needs are and which programs best suit those needs. For example, if you were looking for funding to start a new business dealing with automotive parts, it would be a waste of time.

   Included in this book are more than 100 grant and loan sources to get you started fast. Just follow the easy instructions and in no time at all you should able to obtain all the cash you need.

## Table of Contents

The Secret Book of Free Money

## Your Personality Traits

Most people head off to work for someone else each day. By purchasing this guide you have taken the first step to marching to your own drum. If you are starting your own business, there are certain personality traits that are needed for success. Take a moment and honestly answer the following questions:

Yes No

\_\_\_ \_\_\_ Are you a self-starter? (Self-motivated)

\_\_\_ \_\_\_ Are you organized?

\_\_\_ \_\_\_ Are you ready to take responsibility for your income?

\_\_\_ \_\_\_ Can you stick to your goals through adversity?

\_\_\_ \_\_\_ Are you prepared to wait several months to make a profit?

\_\_\_ \_\_\_ Does a market exist for your product?

\_\_\_ \_\_\_ Do you know how to sell enough of your product or service?

\_\_\_ \_\_\_ Do you like to think ahead and plan for your future, then make it happen?

\_\_\_ \_\_\_ Are you able to work long hours for extended periods of time?

Although nothing is guaranteed, if you answered yes to most of these questions you may possess what it takes to start your own business. If most of your answers were no, then you should take a step back and decide if this is for you and are you ready to work hard to change your ways to develop the traits necessary to start your own business.

# Billions of Dollars are Available

There are many Corporate, Individual, Foundation and Government grant programs. Billions of dollars are given away each and every year. In recent years the government has given away more than 200 billion dollars in different programs.

The Federal Government gives many types of grants, low interest loans and loan guarantees. These programs are good for the economy and good for those who apply and receive the benefits of these programs. The government has many programs to help individuals and families. These programs include housing subsidies including homeowner loan guarantees, grants to start or expand businesses, especially in economically depressed areas, subsidies for farmers, community related projects and a host of other areas.

Programs exist to enhance and encourage the study of the arts. You could get paid to produce a work of art. Why not apply for a grant? A large amount of cash is given to encourage minority business ventures, including businesses owned by women. All of these programs lead to strong growth in the economy.

Many of the same type of programs exist in the private sector. There are so many programs set up to encourage individuals and groups to start or expand their own businesses. Some of the most overlooked programs are sponsored by the national business chains. Many nationally recognized businesses are franchises started with minimal cash outlay. Don't overlook them. Take this opportunity to review the grant and loan programs available to virtually everyone. We're sure one exists that will suit your needs.

Many of the programs in this book are aimed at those who do not qualify for conventional financing. Both the government and private industry want to encourage business growth for people who cannot get help and/or financing from the banks. In order to qualify for some of the programs outlined in this you must be turned down by a bank. So don't think you won't have a chance.

There are over 2500 Grant making organizations that give away billions of dollars to people just like you. With this book you now have a powerful tool for getting free or low cost money. You have to make a commitment to use it. Read through this book thoroughly and take action. By taking a chance and applying for some of the grants and loans in this book you have nothing to lose and much to gain.

# Credit

Believe it or not, many programs are designed for those who cannot obtain traditional financing. In some programs identified in this book (of course!) you will not even be considered <u>unless you have been turned down by a bank first!</u> So if your credit history is not perfect, don't despair, you can still obtain cash.

Traditional lenders judge you by what appears on your credit report. If you have less than favorable items, i.e. late payments, judgments, charge-offs, bankruptcies, etc., it will be difficult to obtain a loan from conventional sources like a bank or credit union. This information has a profound impact on your ability to obtain any type of credit. It is essential that you make sure the information on your credit report is accurate and up to date. Over the course of time information may make its way onto your credit report that is incorrect.

Getting your credit report cleared of inaccuracies is not an easy task. Because these reports are so powerful Congress passed laws over twenty years ago to protect individuals against creditors and credit bureaus. The Fair Credit Reporting Act sets guidelines that must be followed. The best way to start is to get a copy of your credit report. Under the guidelines of the Fair Credit Reporting Act you may obtain a copy of your credit report anytime.

Credit reporting agencies or bureaus, usually charge around $15 to get a copy. You can receive a copy for free if you've been turned down for credit, as long as you request a copy in writing within 30 days of the denial. There are a number of credit bureaus however the larger ones are the best place to look for your records. You can write to one of the address below and request a copy of your credit report.

Equifax
P.O. Box 740256          (equifax.com)
Atlanta, GA 30374

TRW
6201 Powers Ferry Rd. # 200          (experian.com)
Atlanta, GA 30339

TRW
P.O. Box 749029          (experian.com)
Dallas, TX 75374

TRW
505 City Parkway West # 110          (experian.com)
Orange, CA 92667

(In case of multiple offices, write to the location nearest you)

Each time you apply for credit, an inquiry is run by the creditor and automatically reported to the credit bureau. No one is allowed to run a credit report without the permission of the person seeking credit. Get a copy of your report check to see if any inquiries were made without your authorization. Too many inquiries without opening a file could be looked upon in a negative way by a creditor. Inquiries stay on your record for one year.

Dispute old files in order to have them removed. Check to make certain if any derogatory items are present on your report, they are removed in a timely manner. Bankruptcies must be removed after ten years. All other negative items such as liens, judgments, late payments, charge-offs, etc., must be removed after seven years.

Next, you should verify all items listed in your name. Often information is recorded and you have no idea what the creditor is referring to. This is especially occurs if you have a common name. Credit Bureaus regularly mix up files. One case came in listing the holder of the account as have being deceased for eight years. Much to the surprise of the bank, not only was he alive but the person wrongly listed in this particular gentlemen's credit report was forty-one years older and had never lived within 2000 miles of the address listed on the report. Had the individual not challenged his credit report, he surely would have been continually rejected for credit, probably forever. There are many different cases involving mistakes on credit reports. It's up to you to check for accuracy on your credit report and to hound the credit bureau and the reporting agency until the problem has been resolved in a satisfactory manner.

The seven steps to improving your credit report:

Get a copy of the report. Request one from one of the previous listed credit agencies. (It's free if you've been turned down within the last 30 days). Verify everything listed on your report. Even your name could be wrong! Check the entire report carefully. Name, address, social security numbers, employment history, etc. A one-digit error on any item can mean the difference between approval or being denied credit.

Formally dispute all errors. Write a letter to the bureau explaining the error and let them know how detrimental these errors are and how important it is to correct them immediately. Only the reporting creditor can add or remove an item from your file. Once you dispute an item, the credit bureau must contact the creditor to verify the information. If the creditor fails to respond, then the credit bureau will remove the item in question. Often the reporting creditor is too busy to respond.

Challenges to legitimate negative items can also be very helpful. Letters denying judgments, charge-offs, bankruptcies, repossessions will be investigated almost every time they are received. If at any time a creditor does not verify the reported information, the credit bureau will remove the disputed item.

Contact creditors directly. Any remaining unfavorable items can be negotiated and removed by contacting each creditor and making arrangements to settle the outstanding balances. Decide how much you realistically can pay. Make sure you can afford to pay the settled upon amount. Most creditors would prefer to get least some of the money owed to them.

Minimize the negative information still on your credit report by adding a consumer statement. By law, you may add a statement up to 100 words to "explain" the reasons behind negative information contained in your credit history. Contact the previously mentioned credit bureaus for full details.

Add positive information to your credit file. In some instances various creditors will not report favorable items to your credit report. Small banks and some smaller credit companies along with doctors, utility companies and even some small department stores don't normally take the time to report information. It's up to you to make certain that the good information is also listed on your credit report. Again you should contact the credit bureaus for details.

## How To Get An Unsecured Personal Loan With Bad Credit

An unsecured loan is money lent to you on just your signature. When you sign the loan agreement, you promise to pay. In order to get a personal loan you have to understand how the financial institutions think. Most lenders use virtually the same guidelines with minor adjustments. Financial institutions are in business to make money. They make money by lending you money. You are important to their business success. Lenders are most interested in two things: Can you pay them back and will you pay them back.? Your income must be enough to support the payments that would be due. Lenders use a debt ratio to determine if you can afford to make the required payments. Your ability to pay is measured by several factors. (Your income, minus your outstanding debts). To calculate your debt ratio, total your monthly debt, (car payments, rent or mortgage, personal loans, alimony, etc.). Include the expected loan payment you are applying for. Take that figure and divide it by the monthly income. Most banks will not lend if the ratio is over 50%. Whether or not you get the loan depends on the ratio you get from your lender. Your willingness to repay is based upon your past credit history. If you demonstrated a good payment record in the past, a lender will figure you will continue your good record in the future. With signature loans, (no collateral) lenders can only threaten to harm your credit record. So if your repayment record is already bad, the lender usually won't take the risk.

### Where to Apply

If your credit is good and your debt ratio is low you can get credit in almost any place. Chances are your mailbox is filled with offers to get new credit cards, switch to lower rate credit cards, upgrade to "gold" cards and a host of gimmicks designed to get your business.

If your credit rating is less than favorable it is more of a challenge to get credit cards. If you never had credit, the best course of action to establish credit is to first get a department store, gas station credit card or a finance company credit card. You will pay more interest. Try to get at least two of these types of cards. Establish a good record and major credit cards will follow. If you do not have good credit it is still possible to get signature loans. Finance companies are usually willing to take more lending risks. They make high-risk loans that banks and credit unions won't. The lending rules of finance companies are less strict however, you'll pay higher interest rates. Usually, much higher! When you are trying to re-establish credit they are usually the only ones who will take a chance with a high-risk account so, you must accept the higher interest rates.

The following is a list of some of the major finance companies. Please check with each company to determine their specific lending policy. Check your local telephone directory for the offices nearest you.


AVCO Financial  http://avcofinance.com/

AVCO generally makes unsecured loans up to $5000. They are considered one of the easier lenders to qualify for. However, the interest rates they charge are usually high. AVCO usually does not approve loans for persons with prior bankruptcies. They will accept slow payments less than 60 days. Loan rates can be as high as 22%. AVCO also offers second mortgages and home equity lines of credit.


Beneficial Finance          https://www.beneficial.com/

Beneficial offers unsecured credit lines generally up to $5000 for up to 60 months. Home equity lines of credit are also offered with either fixed or adjustable rates. They generally require some other form of credit and make loans on persons with debt ratios of around 40%. If you made slow payments in the past then you will need to explain the circumstances and show the situation has been corrected.

Household Finance (HFC) http://www.HFC.com

HFC offers personal loans and home equity loans. The general requirements For loans are two years at the same job and residence and a debt ratio of 40% or less. They have been known to consider those with less than perfect credit as long as a reasonable excuse exists for the problem. As with virtually all companies, loan rates vary depending on your credit situation.

CitiFinancial          http://www.citifinancial.com

CitiFinancial offers unsecured personal loans, home equity lines of credit and homeowner loans. CitiFinancial will consider those with bankruptcies discharged at least two years ago. Most unsecured loans have a maximum of $3500 with a debt ratio of 40% or less. Loans for larger amounts are secured by automobiles and boats with clear title. Those loans are usually made up to $5000. Home equity loans are made up to 75% of the value of your house. All loan rates vary depending on your credit rating.


America One Funding          http://www.amone.com

Loans from $1000 to $50,000. Loans over $5000 generally require some form of collateral such as a boat or car. Bankruptcies are usually not accepted. Other credit problems, such as slow payments must be corrected. Points and various fees are charged on home equity loans. Home equity loans are made starting at $6000 and up.

There are many finance companies nationwide. The companies listed above are among the largest. Rates, terms and requirements vary depending upon your individual situation and the company you are dealing with. The descriptions listed above are in no way absolute. They are meant to give a broad overview of what you can expect from finance companies in general. Please "shop" for the best rates at several different companies. Check your local listings for the companies in your area. Call and ask for detailed information.

Loans By Mail

When shopping for a loan by mail be very wary of Loan Brokers. They typically charge a fee just to forward your application to a lending institution. These fees can range up to $300 or more. Save yourself the grief and aggravation and deal directly with the lender. Do not confuse Loan Brokers with Mortgage Brokers. Mortgage Brokers arrange real estate loans and are paid after the real estate deal has been completed. Many Loan Brokers advertise in newspapers across the country. Be very careful of anyone who wants to be paid prior to you getting your loan approved.

## The following companies will consider loans to those with less than perfect credit.

Contact the companies direct and request an application.

Wachovia Bank
Wachovia.com
Customer Service: 800-WACHOVIA (800-922-4684)
Request: Premier Visa / MasterCard
Amounts: $5000-$15000

Citibank
www.citibank.com
Customer Service: 1-800-374-9700
Request: Checking Plus Line of Credit Application
Amount: $500-$15,000 unsecured

Bank of America
www.bankofamerica.com
Customer Service: 1.800.432.1000
Personal Loans: 1.888.457.2543
Request: Selective Line of Credit
Amounts: $3000-$25,000
May consider your loan request even with bankruptcy

SunTrust
www.suntrust.com
Customer Service: 800.SUNTRUST (800.786.8787)
Amounts: $300 and up

BB&T
www.bbt.com
Customer Service: 1-800-BANK-BBT (1-800-226-5228)
Offers free checking

Washington Mutual Bank
http://Wamu.com
Customer Service: (800) 788-7000
Offers free checking

Wells Fargo Bank
http://Wellsfargo.com
Customer Service: 1-800-869-3557

# How To Get A Major Credit Card with No Credit

Ever to try to travel without a major credit card? You will run into major obstacles. It is next to impossible to rent a car or even get a hotel room without one. Most places even want a major credit card as a form of identification. Most travel related businesses don't want to take cash.

Credit cards are safer to deal with and very traceable. Obtaining a major credit Card with bad credit is a little more difficult but, not impossible. The key is to remove as much damaging information as you possibly can from your credit report.

Probably the best you can use a credit card is to keep it on hand for emergencies.

# 3 Different Types of Credit Cards

Bank Issued Credit Cards

The two main bank credit cards are issued by Visa and MasterCard. Each bank sets its own policies regarding issued cards. It is very possible to receive a credit card from one bank even after being turned down by another. These cards are accepted virtually everywhere. Sometimes they are too easy to get and can be hard to keep up with the payments. Because you buy now and pay later, many people don't realize that sooner or the bill will be coming in.

Interest rates vary wildly. Banks are trying to lure the best card holders in with rates as low as 4.9%. Keep in mind that you must read the fine print. These rates are usually good for six months or so and then go back up to the current rates. For those with good credit, the best strategy is to get a low rate credit card and transfer your existing balance off of a higher rate card for the duration of the low rate period. At that point you can transfer balances to a different low rate card. By doing this you can save yourself hundreds of dollars interest if you keep a moderate balance on your credit card.

The difference between the interest on a credit card with a $2000 balance @ 19.8% annual percentage rate (APR) and $2000 @ 4.9% APR is phenomenal. Some banks charge an annual fee while others don't.

Merchant Cards

Issued by individual companies, these cards are good only at the issuing company. Department stores, oil (gasoline) companies, rental car companies, furniture companies, etc. Issue these cards. The purpose is to get you to shop in their stores. Getting one of these cards is easier than a regular credit card.

Travel and Entertainment Cards

Originally marketed towards executives and frequent travelers these cards differ significantly from both Bank Credit Cards and Merchant Cards. Travel and Entertainment cards have no pre-set spending limit. These card offer no financing. You are expected to pay your balance in full at the end of each month. These cards usually charge a higher annual fee than credit cards and the income requirements are generally higher.

If you are just starting out and have little or no credit and no negative credit, then chances are you will or have received a credit application by mail from one or more of the banks. If not, then the strategy to use to establish credit would be to apply for a merchant credit card. As mentioned earlier, these cards are easier to obtain and a great way to get started. As long as you have a job with a steady income, you should be able to get your application approved. When you do purchase an item on your merchant card, pay off the minimum every two weeks instead of once per month. This looks better to the credit companies and should enable you to obtain a major credit card faster.

If you have negative credit your strategy must be different. The best way to re-establish credit would be to start with local stores that offer lay-away programs. This generally helps establish a working relationship with store/credit managers. Purchase an item on lay-away. Pay off the item in four weeks. Then repeat the process two or three times. Make certain you keep all of your receipts. After success several times with this program, apply for a store credit card directly with the credit manager. If you are rejected, ask for an appointment with the person in charge of store credit. Show your good record and receipts from the lay-away purchases. This demonstrates your ability to pay back on items. A good track record should be enough to get you a store card as long as you have a steady income and a permanent residence. If you still cannot obtain a store card then apply for credit through a rent-to-own store. These stores regularly deal with high credit risk customers.

The rent-to-own stores generally charge higher than average prices plus high interest however, some may find that these are the only stores that will extend credit to high credit risk buyers. The added cost would be worth the money in order to re-establish your credit. Compare prices and stay within reason.

Another route to re-establishing credit is through a secure credit card. These cards look identical to regular credit cards however you have pledged a secure deposit with the card-issuing bank. Your card is backed by your deposit. The deposit must stay in the bank (earning interest of course) until your purchase is paid off. Some secured card issuers will allow you to charge up to one and one-half the amount on deposit. For example deposit $500 and charge up to $750.

The following banks are among those who issue secure cards:

Sprint Visa 1-888-280-6617 and mention card code 257M
Bankcard Service Center  (www.1800bankcard.com)
Providian Bank 1-800-356-0011 (www.providian.com)
Bank of Hoven 1-800 777-7735

# Grants

Each year billions are given away in grant programs sponsored by federal, local and private funds. In this section grants are the primary topic however, some programs have both grants and loans available.

What is a Grant?

A grant is money given away and not repaid like a loan. Grants are available from Federal, State and local governments. Grants are also available from private sources. These include public and private foundation grants as well as corporations, trusts and other sources that benefit the community. No matter what grant source you choose, the grant asking process is essentially the same.

The one major secret to obtaining a grant is analyzing organization patterns and practices. You would not contact an organization that caters to non-profit funding if you don't fit their criteria. Each organization has certain standards. Government, state and local grants are fairly uniform in their standards. Private funding sources can adopt rules to fit their own organization objectives.

Grants are usually given away with a specific purpose in mind. Ask for objectives before applying for a grant. Some private foundations make grants to enhance their organization reputation. Many large companies make grants in order to receive free publicity. Let's face it, nearly all grant sources do it for the tax breaks they receive.

Depending on which type of grant you are seeking, you may have to present a grant proposal. Different grant sources have different requirements. Some companies want a full grant package while others only require a simple letter. A full grant package consists of a business plan, including finance statements with future earning projections, and references both personal and business related.

The best way to get started is to send a letter to the organization that you are seeking funds from requesting a copy of their grant proposal guidelines. Once you receive the guidelines follow their instructions as close as possible (certain grant funds are distributed once per year, if you leave out a required item your request will be automatically rejected).

Points to remember:

Write your proposal or Business Plan with the grant maker's goals and objectives in mind. Plan carefully; make your project stand out. Be realistic about funding sources and be ready to prove any statements you make. Grant proposals fail when the grant seeker fails to do his/her homework.

Many private grants are given away to non-profit organizations. You must be a non-profit organization in order to be considered. Check with the IRS and your individual state to determine the requirements to form a non-profit organization. You can also affiliate yourself with a non-profit organization and apply for funds under them. Keep in mind that in order to successfully affiliate yourself or company with a non-profit organization you must demonstrate how they too will benefit. Individual grants are also given away. These are usually awarded to those doing research, education, studying the arts or performing some form of community service.

There are several basic points that must be addressed in any grant proposal. Every grant proposal must begin with a cover letter. The cover letter introduces yourself to the person in charge of making the decision about approving your grant or the head of the grant committee. (Many grants are decided upon by a committee.) Along with introducing yourself, it also introduces your project. The cover letter should be about one page long.

On the next page you begin by briefly stating what your objectives are and how you are going to meet your goals. Follow this up with the body of the proposal. The body is where you explain how you are going to accomplish your mission. You can use surveys, charts, graphs, pictures, figures or any other item that will help clearly explain why you need money and more importantly, why your proposal should be approved over others being considered. Keep in mind that while most organizations give money for many causes, often they set limits to how much they give out or how many grants they give. Make certain that your proposal is backed by a good solid foundation including sound reasoning and realistic expectations. By accomplishing this simple task your proposal may be approved ahead of another who is missing these key ingredients. The body can be as short as one page, depending upon what your objectives are. Get to the point. Don't ramble on with unnecessary filler. It will not help. For example, a letter for a senior citizens center proposal will state who you are and why you should be chosen to receive a grant for this project.

It will then state in detail how the funds are to be used. At this point you may use charts, graphs, etc., to illustrate your financial picture. For instance, lets say you applied for $50,000 in grant funds for your project. State how much it will cost per month for rent, i.e. $1000, utilities, materials to redecorate and furnish the facility, i.e. $10,000 and put the remainder into a bank account to pay the bills associated with operating the center.

Explain how the newly refurbished area will be completed, maybe with the help of some volunteers to paint and decorate. In your objective you would state that you are seeking to provide local senior citizens with a safe environment where they can come and enjoy the company of other seniors and have hot, nutritional meals each day.

End your proposal with an appendix that will include your personal resume (if required) outlining your experience in the field you have chosen, certifications and tax exempt forms (if required), affiliations with related groups and list former projects and accomplishments.

Be sure to include:
* A brief introduction to your idea or concept.
* A description of your financial needs.
* What your objectives are.
* How you will accomplish your objectives.


If for some reason your grant is not approved, you should request an explanation. Write a letter to the organization you applied to and ask why your grant request was denied. The reasons behind the denial can help you in a later request for funding.

Some of the reasons why grant proposals are turned down:
- The grant requester (you) failed to sufficiently demonstrate need.
- The proposal failed to clearly spell out your objectives.
- The grant organization does not have sufficient funds.
- The proposal does not suit the requirements of the organization.

## Finding Grants

Many different sources of grants exist. Finding a grant can be a long a frustrating task, especially for the beginner. There are so many different places to look you can spend months trying to find the one that fits your needs.

The Federal Government provides a wide array of grants for many different purposes. To get the most complete list of grant assistance programs offered by the Federal Government write to the

Superintendent of Documents, Government
Printing Office, Washington, DC. 20503.
www.gpoaccess.gov/

Request a catalog of available assistance programs.

One of the most comprehensive sources of grant information is The Foundation Center. They offer seminars and computerized searches of their extensive databases and directories.

Contact them at: http://foundationcenter.org/
Or write to them at the following addresses:
* New York - 79 Fifth Avenue, New York, NY. 10006,
* Washington -1001, Connecticut Avenue, NW, Washington, DC. 20036
* San Francisco - 312 Sutter Street, San Francisco, CA. 94109.

## Prospect Research

Prospect research is the task of tracking down the widest range of funding targets for your project. You must narrow down these sources, analyze them and their objectives. You can then concentrate on the organizations that closely match your grant criteria. There are no shortcuts in prospect research.

For a list of available government grants, check the following sources:
- Catalog of Federal Domestic Assistance
  http://www.gsa.gov/cfda
also available from the:
Superintendent of Documents
U.S. Government Printing Office, Washington, DC 20402

  Federal Information Center
  http://www.info.gov/
also listed in the white pages of your local telephone book.

- The Congressional Register
  http://www.gpoaccess.gov/
also available at your local library.

- The Federal Register
  http://www.gpoaccess.gov/fr/Index.html
also available at your local library.

**How to Ask for Grant Money**

Your initial contact with a potential grant source is the most important. Whether by telephone, personal visit or letter, remember, you only have one chance to make a first impression. Be certain to request the specific information you need to complete your proposal. Verify the information that you have already gathered, including names, addresses, telephone numbers, etc. Also, be sure to request a copy of their annual report and program guidelines they may have.

Education Grants

Much of the billions of dollars set aside for education go unused because people do not apply. Education grants also come in the form of scholarships. Outlined below are various grants available. Also check with the financial aid officer at the school you are planning to attend as well as the school you are currently in (if applicable).

The most common grants available through the government are:

The Department of Education

One of the largest grant making organizations, the Department of Education offers a wide array of grant programs. Contact them on the web at http://www.ed.gov/ at the office listed below.

Some of the available programs include:
* Basic Educational Opportunity Grants
* Foreign Language and Area Studies Research Grants
* Fulbright-Hays Training Grants
* Public Service Education Institutional Grants
* Graduate and Professional Opportunities
* Minority Access to Research Careers

The Department of Education offices are located at 400 Maryland Avenue, SW.
Washington, DC 20202.

Pell Grants - (once known as BEOG) - used for undergraduate studies. The awarded amounts are based upon your income and the cost of your studies.
http://www.ed.gov/programs/fpg/index.html

Perkins Loans - (once known as National Direct Student Loans). Available for both undergraduate and graduate studies.
http://www.ed.gov/programs

SEOG - (Supplementary Educational Opportunity Grants) - based upon need and college costs. The above educational funding programs are applied for through the school you wish to attend.

http://www.ed.gov/programs/fseog

GSL - (Guaranteed Student loans) - available through many banks and used for college undergraduate and graduate studies, trade and technical schools.


For additional grants for trade and technical schools as well as college

Funding contact:
The Office of Education
The Department of Health, Education and Welfare
330 Independence Avenue
Washington, DC. 20506
http://www.ed.gov/

Be sure to state your field of interest in order to receive the necessary information. In addition to government sponsored financial aid programs for education, private funding is available. Listed below are some of the private funding sources for educational aid.

Additional sources can be found in your local library and through the school you are planning to attend.

Independent College Fund of New York
11 E 44th Street
New York, NY. 10017
http://www.icf-ny.org/

Grants for the Study of the Arts

Through the National Endowment for the Arts money is available for the artists. These include but, are not limited to studies in art, dance, design, literature, Music, opera, radio, film, television and theater. The easiest way to secure a grant is to become affiliated with professional and non-profit organizations. These grant programs are designed to help those already established as well as beginning artists. For more information contact: http://www.nea.gov/ or at the main offices:

The National Endowment for the Arts
2401 E Street NW.
Washington, DC. 20506

STRATEGIES FOR OBTAINING GRANTS

Very often the best strategy for obtaining a grant is to join together with an individual or group with similar interests or goals. By banding together and forming an ad-hoc committee, the funding seekers create an increased sense of credibility. If your grant request is for some form of community project you could form a nonprofit organization. There are several advantages to forming this type of organization however, the guidelines are very strict. Check with your local Internal Revenue Service Office (http://www.irs.gov) or local business development agency for all of the  information regarding requirements.

You may also want to incorporate. Corporations look stronger on paper and may receive an edge over an individual when applying for grants.

GOVERNMENT GRANTS

It is estimated that anywhere from $10 - 50 billion dollars per year are given away in government grants. The following list includes government grants listed by agency. These grants are open and available to corporations, both non-profit and profit as well as individuals. Contact each in order to receive a grant application kit.

Some corporations, unions, and fraternal organizations provide education financial aid in the form of grants to members' families. Don't overlook them as a source of aid.

Department of Agriculture
http://www.usda.gov/

* Agriculture Conservation Program
* Basic and Applied Agriculture Research Grants
* Competitive Research Grants
* Emergency Conservation Programs
* Farm Labor Housing Grants
* Technical and Supervisory Assistance Grants

Most states also have an agriculture office. Check your state listings.
You can also write to the Department of Agriculture at either of the following addresses:

- Main Headquarters: 14th Street and Independence Avenue SW.
  Washington DC 20250
- Northeast Region: Room 333 Admin. Bldg. Beltsville Agriculture Research Ctr.
  Beltsville, MD 20705
- North Central Region: 2000 West Pioneer Parkway, Peoria, IL 61614
- Southern Region: 701 Loyola Avenue, PO Box 53326 New Orleans, LA 70153
- Western Region: 2850 Telegraph Road, Berkeley, CA 94705

Department of Commerce
http://www.commerce.gov/

The Department of Commerce sponsors several different programs that are open individuals and non-profit organizations. One of the largest program categories includes Minority Business Development. Many of their programs are administered through the Economic Development Administration. You can go online or write to your nearest office for complete details.

The Department of Commerce headquarters is located at 14th Street and
Constitution Avenue,
NW. Washington DC. 20230.
Most states also have a commerce office. Check your state listings.

The Economic Development Administration is also a good resource. You can access them via the web at http://www.eda.gov/.

They also have regional offices.
* Atlantic: The Federal Building 600 Arch Street, Philadelphia, PA 19106
* Southeast: Suite 700, 1365 Peachtree St., NE. Atlanta, GA 30309
* Midwest: 175 W. Jackson Blvd. Suite A-1630, Chicago, IL 60604
* Southwest: Suite 600 American Bank Tower, 221 West 6th Street, Austin, TX 78701
* Rocky Mountain: Suite 505, Title Building 907 17th St, Denver CO 80202
* West: 1700 Westlake Avenue North, Suite 500, Seattle, WA 98109

Department of Health and Human Services

http://www.hhs.gov/

The Department of Health and Human Services offers various types of grants primarily for medical research. Contact them and request a copy of their grant guidelines.

Their offices are located at:
* John F. Kennedy Federal Building, Government Center, Boston, MA 02203
* Department of Health and Human Services, 26 Federal Plaza, Room 3835,NY, NY 10007
* Department of Health and Human Services, 3535 Market Street, Philadelphia, PA 19101
* Department of Health and Human Services, 101 Marietta Tower Building Atlanta, GA 30323
* Department of Health and Human Services, 300 Wacker Drive, Chicago, IL 60606
* Department of Health and Human Services, 1200 Main Tower Building, Dallas TX 75202
* Department of Health and Human Services, 601 East 12th St. Kansas City, MO 64106
* Federal Office Building, 1961 Stout Street, Denver CO 80294
* Federal Office Building, United Nations Plaza: San Francisco, CA 94102

Department of the Interior
http://www.doi.gov/

The Department of the Interior is comprised of several different agencies which administer grant programs independently of each other. These agencies include the Bureau of Indian Affairs, the Bureau of Land Management, Fish and Wildlife Service, Forest Service and the National Park Service. Some of the available grants include water research grants, wildlife research grants, Native American programs, etc. The Department of Interior headquarters is located at 18th and C Streets, NW. Wash, DC 20202.

Department of Labor

http://www.dol.gov/

The Department of Labor sponsors grant programs for small non-profit organizations. Contact them online or directly at one of the regional offices below.
Ask for a grant package.

* John F. Kennedy Building, Government Center, Boston MA 02203
* 1515 Broadway, Rm. 3730, New York, NY 10036
* P.O. Box 8796, Philadelphia, PA 19101
* 1371 Peachtree St. NE. Rm. 405, Atlanta, GA 30309
* 230 South Dearborn St., Chicago, IL 60604

\* 555 Griffin Square Bldg., Griffin and Young St., Dallas, TX 75202
\* Federal Bldg. Rm. 1000, 911 Walnut St., Kansas City, MO 64106
\* Federal Office Bldg. 909 First Ave., Seattle, WA 98174

National Endowment for the Humanities

NEH grants include scholarships for Higher Education, Mid Career Programs, Promotion of the humanities as well as a host of subjects. For further information contact them directly at: http://www.neh.gov/

National Endowment for the Humanities
806 15th Street, NW.
Washington, DC 20506

An excellent place to start your search for grants is through a grant making association. You can write to them directly and request information about the programs they administer. I've also included a table of grant making associations in the back of this guide.

# BUSINESS FINANCING

Starting a business can be a scary venture. The best way to get started is to do your research thoroughly. Without the proper research you might as well be throwing money out of the window. You know sooner or later its going to land but, you don't know where. If you have tons of money to risk (then you wouldn't be reading this book) then just go for it. The rest of us need to follow the sensible approach. In this section we will discuss some of the many different options associated with raising capital to start or expand your own business. I will detail how to get started as well as who can help you. Whether you are just starting out or expanding an existing business don't overlook one of the most successfully used methods of raising capital.

Regardless of your current financial situation a Venture Capitalist will consider a request for capital from virtually anyone, as long as your proposal is sound. Many companies were started with other people's money!

A Venture Capital Firm is an organization with cash looking to invest in up and coming business usually for a healthy return or a piece of the business. Venture Capital firms have been providing millions of dollars to start many different kinds of business. Many of these firms advertise in the local papers. In the Business Opportunity section or nearby classifieds section check for advertisements like:"Wealthy investor seeks local offers. Have $1M to invest. Call XXX-XXX-XXXX for additional information." Coincidentally some businesses seeking investors have also taken out advertisements for capital. These ads may say something like: "Investor needed for manufacturing company. 12% return on $25,000. Call XXX-XXX-XXXX."

The following pages contain capital organizations, small business investment companies (SBIC's), minority enterprise small business investment companies (MESBIC's), and firms specializing in small business funding. There are many, many more. Additional information is available through your local library.

# Small Business Investment Companies (SBICs)

## Alabama

Founders Investment Banking, LLC
2204 Lakeshore Dr, Ste 425
Birmingham, AL. 35209
(205) 949-2043        http://www.foundersib.com/

First SBIC of Alabama
Mobile, Alabama
205-476-0700 (voice)
205-476-0026 (fax)

FJC Growth Capital Corp.
165 West Park Loop NW
Huntsville, AL 35806-1745       http://www.fjcgrowth.com

Alabama Capital Corporation
16 Midtown Park E
Mobile, AL 36606-4140
(251) 476-0700

Hickory Venture Capital Corp.
301 Washington Street, NW
Suite 301
Huntsville AL, 35801
(256) 539-1931
(256) 539-5130 fax       info@hvcc.com

## Alaska

No companies listed

## Arizona

FBS Venture Capital Co.
6900 E. Camelback Rd. Suite 452
Scottsdale, AZ 85251

Grayhawk Venture Fund I, L.P.
Sherman Chu, Contact
5050 North 40th Street, Suite 310
Phoenix, AZ 85018
Phone:    (602) 956-8700      Fax:(602) 956-8080       Email:     schu@gvp.us

Magnet Capital, L.P.
3550 North Central Ave., Suite 1400
Phoenix, AZ 85012
Phone:    (602) 222-4801      Fax:(602) 222-4807       Email:
info@magnetcapital.com

**Arkansas**

Diamond State Ventures, L.P.
Joe T. Hays, Contact
200 South Commerce Street
Suite 400
Little Rock, AR  72201-1728
Phone:      (501) 374-9247          Fax:(501) 374-9425                    Email: jhays@arcapital.com

Small Business Investment Capital, Inc.
John R. Mills, President
12103 Interstate 30
Mail: P.O. Box 3627
Little Rock, AR  72203
Phone:      (501) 455-6599          Fax:(501) 455-6556          Email:      jmills@afslr.com

**California**

American River Ventures, L.P.
Attention: Sher Pastino
2270 Douglas Blvd., Suite 212
Roseville, CA  95661
Phone:      (916) 780-2828          Fax:(916) 780-5443          Email:
plans@arventures.com

Bank of America Ventures
Hayley Hoad, Manager, Administration
950 Tower Lane, Suite 700
Foster City, CA  94404
Phone:      (650) 378-6000          Fax:(650) 378-6040          Email:
               hayley@scalevp.com

Bentley Capital   (SSBIC)
John Hung, President
290 7th Avenue
San Francisco, CA  94118-
Phone:      (415) 751-1608          Fax:(415) 751-2110          Email:      lc-chan@att.net

Celerity Partners SBIC, L.P.
11111 Santa Monica Blvd., Suite 1127
Los Angeles, CA  90025
Fax:        (310) 268-1712                                        Email:
kraus@celeritypartners.com

Draper Associates, a California LP
Timothy C. Draper, President
2882 Sand Hill Road #150
Menlo Park, CA  94025
Phone:      (650) 233-9000          Fax:(650) 234-8584          Email:      karen@dfj.com

Draper-Richards L.P.
William Draper III, President
50 California Street,
Suite 2925
San Francisco, CA 94111
Phone:     (415) 616-4050          Fax:(415) 616-4060          Email:
Cynthia@draperrichards.com

Emergence Capital Partners SBIC, L.P.
Gordon Ritter, Contact
160 Bovet Road, Suite 300
San Mateo, CA 94402
Phone:     (650) 573-3100          Fax:(650) 573-3119          Email:  gritter@emergencecap.com

Far East Capital Corp.
350 S. Grand Ave., Suite 4100
Los Angeles, CA 90071
Phone:     (213) 830-2430          Fax:(213) 830-2415          Email:  Bowen.Chang@FENB-
US.com

GCG SBIC Investors, L.P.
111 Sutter Street, Suite 1950
San Francisco, CA 94104
Phone:     (415) 273-3506          Fax:(415) 362-3311

GKM SBIC, L.P.
Jonathan R. Bloch, Contact
11150 Santa Monica Blvd., Suite 825
Los Angeles, CA 90025
Phone:     (310) 268-2623          Fax:(310) 268-0870  Email:        jbloch@gkmventures.com

Hamilton BioVentures, LP
Richard Crosby, Contact
990 Highland Drive, Suite 314
Solana Beach, CA 92075-
Phone:     (858) 314-2350          Fax:(858) 314-2355 Email:rcrosby@hamiltonbioventures.com

Hercules Technology II, L.P.
Scott Harvey, Contact
525 University Avenue, Suite 700
Palo Alto, CA 94301
Phone:     (847) 867-1953          Fax:(866) 828-6687  Email:      sharvey@herculestech.com

Horizon Ventures Fund II, LP
Debby Schilling, Contact
4 Main Street, Suite 50
Los Altos, CA 94022
Phone:     (650) 917-4100          Fax:(650) 917-4109  Email:       debby@horizonvc.com

Housatonic Equity Investors SBIC, L.P.
Barry Reynolds, Will Thorndike
44 Montgomery Street, Suite 4010
San Francisco, CA 94104
Phone:      (415) 955-9020          Fax:(415) 981-0617
                  Email:breynolds@housatonicpartners.com

Huntington Capital, L.P.
Morgan Miller and Barry Wilson, Contacts
11988 El Camino Real, Suite 160
San Diego, CA 92130
Phone:      (858) 259-7654          Fax:(858) 259-0074    Email:  susan@huntingtoncapital.com
www.huntingtoncapital.com
Labrador Ventures V-B, L.P.
Sean Foote, Contact
101 University Avenue, 4th Floor
Palo Alto, CA 94301
Phone:      (650) 366-6000          Fax:(650) 366-6430    Email:      mpollasky@labrador.com

Marwit Capital Company, L.P.
Chris Britt, President
100 Bayview Circle
Suite 550
Newport Beach, CA 92660
Phone:      (949) 861-3636          Fax:(949) 861-3637    Email:      mckay@marwit.com

Montreux Equity Partners II SBIC, L.P.
Daniel K. Turner III, General Partner
3000 Sand Hill Road
Building 1, Suite 260
Menlo Park, CA 94025-7073
Phone:      (650) 234-1200          Fax:(650) 234-1250    Email:      dturner@montreuxequity.com

Novus Ventures II, L.P.
Daniel D. Tompkins, Managing GP
20111 Stevens Creek Blvd., Suite 130
Cupertino, CA 95014
Phone:      (408) 252-3900          Fax:(408) 252-1713    Email:      glahann@novusventures.com

Opportunity Capital Corporation  (SSBIC)
J. Peter Thompson, President
2201 Walnut Avenue, Suite 210
Fremont, CA 94538
Phone:      (510) 795-7000          Fax:(510) 494-5439    Email:      rcg@ocpcapital.com

Outlook Ventures III, L.P.
Carl Nichols, Contact
135 Main Street, Suite 1350
San Francisco, CA 94105

Phone:     (415) 547-0000      Fax:(415) 547-0010    Email:     carl@outlookventures.com

Pacific Mezzanine Fund, L.P.
Nathan W. Bell, General Partner
2 Theatre Square, Suite 210
Orinda, CA  94563-
Phone:     (510) 595-9800      Fax:(510) 595-9801    Email:     mcs@pacmezz.com

Peninsula Equity Partners SBIC, L.P.
Gregory C. Ennis, Contact
3000 Sand Hill Road
Building 3, Suite 125
Menlo Park, CA  94025
Phone:     (650) 854-0314      Fax:(650) 854-0670    Email:     ennis@peninsulaequity.com

Positive Enterprises, Inc.   (SSBIC)
Kwok Szeto, President
1489 Webster Street, Suite 228
San Francisco, CA  94115
Phone:     (415) 885-6600      Fax:(415) 928-6363    Email:   nszeto@pei-sba.com

Red Rock Ventures SBIC III, L.P.
Laura Gwosden , Contact
180 Lytton Avenue
Palo Alto, CA  94301
Phone:     (650) 325-3111      Fax:(650) 853-7044    Email: lgwosden@redrockventures.com

Rembrandt Venture Partners II, L.P.
Gerald S. Casilil, Contact
2200 Sand Hill Road, Suite 160
Menlo Park, CA  94025
Phone:     (650) 326-7070      Fax:(650) 326-3780    Email:     jcasilli@rembrandtvc.com

Rustic Canyon Ventures SBIC, L.P.
Paul Notaras, Contact
2425 Olympic Blvd., Suite 6050 W
Santa Monica, CA  90404
Phone:     (310) 998-8050      Fax: (310) 998-8061   Email:     paul@rusticcanyon.com

SAIL Venture Partners, L.P.
David Jones, Contact
600 Anton Blvd., Suite 1010
Costa Mesa, CA  92626
Phone:     (714) 241-7500      Fax:(714) 241-7505    Email:     djones@sailvc.com

Shepherd Ventures II, L.P.
George C. Kenney, Contact

12250 El Camino Real, Suite 116
San Diego, CA  92130-
Phone:       (858) 509-4744       Fax:(858) 509-3662    Email:     olga@shepherdventures.com

Sorrento Growth Partners I, L.P.
Robert Jaffe, Manager
4370 La Jolla Village Drive, Suite 1040
San Diego, CA  92122
Phone:       (858) 452-3100   Fax:(858) 452-7607   Email: ecampbell@sorrentoventures.com

St. Cloud Capital Partners, L.P.
10866 Wilshire Blvd., Suite 1450
Los Angeles, CA  90024
Phone:       (310) 475-2700       Fax:(310) 475-0550    Email:ctennyson@stcloudcapital.com

Stone Canyon Venture Partners, L.P.
Mike Seibert, Contact
150 Barrington Place
Los Angeles, CA  90049
Phone:       (310) 432-5180       Fax:(310) 861-0101    Email:     mseibert@scvp.com

Telegraph Hill Partners SBIC, L.P.
Robert G. Shepler, Contact
360 Post Street, Suite 601
San Francisco, CA  94108
Phone:       (415) 765-6980       Fax:(415) 765-6983    Email:     rgs@thpartners.net

TeleSoft Partners II SBIC, L.P.
Arjun Gupta, Manager
Metro Center Tower
950 Tower Lane, Suite 1600
Foster City, CA  94404
Phone:       (650) 358-2500       Fax:(650) 358-2501    Email:     telesoft@telesoftvc.com

## Colorado

Appian Ventures SBIC I, L.P.
Phillip Dignan, Contact
1512 Larimer Street, Suite 200
Denver, CO  80202-
Phone:       (303) 830-2450       Fax:(303) 830-2449    Email:     phillip@appianvc.com

Roaring Fork Capital SBIC, L.P.
Eugene McColley, Contact
5350 South Roslyn Street, Suite 380
Greenwood Villag, CO  80111-2124
Phone:       (303) 694-1300       Fax:(303) 694-1181    Email:
             tiffany@roaringforkcapital.com

Vista Ventures Advantage, LP
Catharine M. Merigold, Contact
1011 Walnut Street, Suite 410
Boulder, CO 80302
Phone:     (303) 543-5716          Fax:(303) 543-5717     Email:     catharine@vistavc.com

## Connecticut

AB SBIC, Inc.
Michael A. Bozzuto, President
275 School House Road
Cheshire, CT 06410
Phone:     (203) 250-5201          Fax:(203) 250-2954     Email:     lablamsky@bozzutos.com

Altus Capital Partners SBIC, L.P.
Russell Greenberg, Contact
10 Wright Street, Suite 110
Westport, CT 06880
Phone:     (203) 429-2006          Fax:(203) 429-2010 Email:
          rgreenberg@altuscapitalpartners.com

Brookside Pecks Capital Partners, L.P.
David D. Buttolph, Corey Sclar;  Contact
80 Field Point Road
Greenwich, CT 06830
Phone:     (203) 618-0202          Fax:(203) 618-0984     Email:     dbuttolph@brooksidegrp.com

Cygnet Capital Partners L.P. SBIC
Owen S. Crihfield, Contact
c/o Hamilton Robinson LLC
281 Tresser Blvd., 4th Floor, Suite 1000
Stamford, CT 06901
Phone:     (203) 602-0011          Fax:(203) 602-2206     Email:     osc@hrco.com

Equinox Capital SBIC, L.P.
Steven C. Rodger, Contact
41 West Putnam Avenue
Greenwich, CT 06830
Phone:     (203) 622-1605          Fax:(203) 622-4684     Email:     scr@equinoxcapitalinc.com

First New England Capital 2, L.P.
Richard Klaffky, Manager
100 Pearl Street
Hartford, CT 06103
Phone:     (860) 293-3333          Fax:(860) 293-3338     Email:     rklaffky@fnec.com

GreenLeaf Capital, L.P.
Michael B. Cowan, Contact
130 Main Street

New Canaan, CT 06840
Phone: (203) 716-6106 Fax:(203) 716-6206 Email: mcowan@whitney.com

Ironwood Equity Fund LP
Marc A. Reich, Contact
55 Nod Road
c/o Ironwood Capital Advisors LLC
Avon, CT 06001
Phone: (860)409-2101 Fax: (860) 409-2120 Email: reich@ironwoodcap.com

Ironwood Mezzanine Fund, L.P.
Marc Reich, President, Contact
55 Nod Road
c/o Ironwood Capital Advisors LLC
Avon, CT 06001
Phone: (860) 409-2101 Fax:(860) 409-2120 Email: reich@ironwoodcap.com

JHW Greentree Capital, L.P.
Michael B. Cowan, Contact
130 Main Street
New Canaan, CT 06840
Phone: (203) 716-6106 Fax:(203) 716-6206 Email: mcowan@whitney.com

Madison Investment Partners II, L.P.
Susan Goodrich, Contact
82 Bradley Road
Madison, CT 06443
Phone: (203) 949-0400 Fax:(203) 245-6945 Email: sgoodrich@madisonpartners.com

Marketing 1 to 1 Ventures, L.P.
Bruce Blasnik, Contact
One Stamford Landing
Suite 101
Stamford, CT 06902
Phone: (203) 325-4000 Fax:(203) 967-8733 Email: bruceb@1to1ventures.com

MSR I SBIC, L.P.
Daniel A. Levinson
120 Post Road West, Suite 101
Westport, CT 06880
Phone: (203) 227-5320 Fax:(203) 227-5312 Email: mt@mainstreetresources.com

RFE Investment Partners V, L.P.
James A. Parsons, General Partner
36 Grove Street
New Canaan, CT 06840
Phone: (203 ) 966-2800 Fax:(203) 966-3109 Email: djuricic@rfeip.com

RFE VI SBIC, L.P.

James Parsons, Managing Member.
36 Grove Street
New Canaan, CT  06840
Phone:      (203) 966-2800         Fax:(203) 966-3109    Email:    djuricic@rfeip.com

Saugatuck Capital Company, L.P. IV, SBIC
Frank Hawley, Thomas Berardino
One Canterbury Green
Stamford, CT  06901
Phone:      (203) 348-6669         Fax:(203) 324-6995    Email:
                TBerardino@saugatuckcapital.com

TD Lighthouse Capital Fund, L.P.
Joan Neuscheler, Contact
c/o Tullis Dickerson Company, Inc.
Two Greenwich Plaza, 4th Floor
Greenwich, CT  06830
Phone:      (203) 629-8700         Fax:(203) 629-9293    Email:
                mmcleish@tullisdickerson.com

Valentis SB, L.P.
Paul M. Jacobi
411 West Putnam Avenue
Greenwich, CT  06830
Phone:      (203) 862-7074         Fax:(203) 862-7374    Email:    pjacob@wexford.com

**Delaware**
Inflection Point Ventures II, L.P.
Jeffrey A. Davison, Contact
1 Innovation Way, Suite 500
Newark, DE  19711
Phone:      (302) 452-1120         Fax:(302) 452-1122    Email:    jdavison@inflectpoint.com

Innovation Ventures, L.P.
David J. Freschman, Contact
Three Mill Road, Suite 201
Wilmington, DE  19806
Phone:      (302) 777-1616         Fax:(302) 777-1620    Email:    djf@innovationventures.com

**District of Columbia**
Alpine Equity, L.P.
George McCabe, Contact
1055 Thomas Jefferson Street, NW
Suite 650
Washington, DC  20007-5256
Phone:      (202) 333-7784         Fax:(202) 333-7786    Email:
                george@pinecreekpartners.com

Core Capital Partners, L.P.
William Dunbar, Contact

1401 I Street, NW, Suite 1000
Washington, DC 20005
Phone: (202) 589-0090      Fax:(202) 589-0091    Email:    rklueger@core-capital.com

Grosvenor Special Ventures IV, L.P.
Bruce B. Dunnan
1808 Eye Street, N.W. , Suite 900
Washington, DC 20006
Phone: (202) 861-5650      Fax: (202) 861-5653   Email:    bbd@grosvenorfund.com

Halifax Growth Partners, L.P.
David W. Dupree, Contact
1133 Connecticut Ave., N.W. Suite 725
Washington, DC 20036
Phone: (202) 530-8300      Fax: (202) 296-7133   Email:
        ddupree@thehalifaxgroup.com

## Florida
Banyan Mezzanine Fund, L.P.
John A. Miller, Contact
P.O. Box 45-0963
Miami, FL 33245-0963
Phone: (305) 755-0376      Fax:(305) 755-0377    Email:
        jmiller@banyanmezzanine.com

BOCF, LLC
Steven F. Lux
707 Azeele Street
Tampa, FL 33606
Phone: (813) 223-9335      Fax:(813) 221-6453    Email:    sflux@stonehengecapital.com

CapitalSouth Partners Fund I, L.P.
David Reed
712 South Oregon Avenue, Suite 200
Tampa, FL 33606-
Phone: (813) 202-8128      Fax:(813) 835-4197

KLH Capital, L.P.
Mark J. Hunter, Contact
101 E. Kennedy Blvd., Suite 3925
Tampa, FL 33602
Phone: (813) 222-8000      Fax: (813) 222-8001   Email:    www.KLHCapital.com

Market Capital Corp.
Eugene C. Langford, President
1715 W. Cleveland Street
Tampa, FL 33606
Phone:    (813) 251-6055        Fax: (813) 251-1900   Email:    pcaskey@langfordhill.com

Power Equities, Inc.
Maureen Beavers
50 N. Laura Street, 9th Floor
Jacksonville, FL 32202
Phone:    (904) 791-7601        Fax:(904) 791-7516

**Georgia**
EGL/NatWest Equity Partners USA, L.P.
Salvatore Massaro, Manager
3495 Piedmont Road
Building 11, Suite 412
Atlanta, GA 30305
Phone:    (404) 949-8303        Fax:(404) 795-0976   Email:    samassaro@eglholdings.com

Global Capital Funding Group, L.P.
Mike Brown, Contact
106 Colony Park Drive, Suite 900
Cumming, GA 30040
Phone:    (678) 947-0028        Fax:(678) 947-6499   Email:    msb@gcaltd.com

Salem Capital Partners II, L.P.
600 Paces Summit
2410 Paces Ferry Road
Atlanta, GA 30339-
Phone:    (770) 805-2320        Fax:(770) 805-2185

**Hawaii**
Pacific Venture Capital, Ltd.
Frank Tokioka
222 South Vineyard Street
PH.1
Honolulu, HI 96813
Phone:    (808) 521-6502        Fax:(808) 521-6541   Email:    dperk@lava.net

**Idaho**
No companies listed

**Illinois**

Aldine SBIC Fund, L.P.
Albert L. Brahm, Contact
30 West Monroe Street, Suite 1310
Chicago, IL 60603
Phone: (312) 346-3950      Fax:(312) 346-3930    Email:    bbrahm@aldinecapital.com

Alpha Capital III SBIC, L.P.
Andrew H. Kalnow, Contact
122 South Michigan Avenue, Suite 1700
Chicago, IL 60603
Phone: (312) 322-9800      Fax:(312) 322-9808    Email:    GaryStark@alphacapital.com

Altus Capital Partners SBIC, L.P.
250 Parkway Drive, Suite 120
Lincolnshire, IL 60069
Phone: (847) 229-0770      Fax:(847) 229-9271

CFB Venture Fund L.P.
Dan W. O' Connell
120 S. Riverside, Suite 2160
Chicago, IL 60606
Phone: (312) 466-9276      Fax:(312) 466-9278

Channel Medical Partners, L.P.
Gregory Shearer, Contact
5750 Old Orchard Road, Suite 310
Skokie, IL 60077
Phone: (847) 779-1550      Fax:(847) 779-1535    Email:    gshearer@chanmed.com

Chicago Venture Partners, L.P.
John Fife, Manager
303 East Wacker Drive, Suite 311
Chicago, IL 60601
Phone: (312) 297-7000      Fax:(312) 819-9701    Email:    general@chicagoventure.com

CIVC Partners Fund, LLC
Christopher J. Perry - Managing Member
191 North Wacker Drive, Suite 1100
Chicago, IL 60606
Phone: (312) 873-7300      Fax:(312) 873-7301    Email:    cperry@civc.com

Continental Illinois Venture Corp.
Terry Perucca, President
231 South LaSalle Street
Chicago, IL 60697
Phone: (312) 828-2287      Fax:(312) 923-0668    Email:
erick.c.christensen@bankofamerica.com

DNJ Leasing II, L.P.
Jeffery S. Pfeffer, Contact
10 S. Wacker Drive, Suite 1840
Chicago, IL  60606
Phone:      (312) 629-2878          Fax:(312) 629-2874      Email:      jspfeffer@capxpartners.com

Fidus Mezzanine Capital, L.P.
Edward H. Ross, Contact
190 S. LaSalle Street, Suite 2140
Chicago, IL  60603-
Phone:      (312) 284-5201          Fax: (312) 914-4456    Email:      eross@fiduspartners.com

GCG SBIC Investors, L.P.
Jeffery Birch, Contact
230 West Monroe Street, Suite 2000
Chicago, IL  60606
Phone:      (312) 849-0008          Fax:(312) 849-0000      Email:
            birch@greyrockcapitalgroup.com

Granite Creek FlexCap I, L.P.
Mark A. Radzik, Contact
222 West Adams, Suite 1980
Chicago, IL  60606
Phone:      (312) 895-4503          Fax:(312) 895-4509      Email:      mark@granitecreek.com

High Street Capital III SBIC, L.P.
Joseph R. Katcha, Contact
11 South LaSalle Street, 5th Floor
Chicago, IL  60603
Phone:      (312) 423-2650          Fax: (312) 423-2655    Email:      jkatcha@highstr.com

Hispania Private Equity, L.P.
Victor L. Maruri, Contact
311 South Wacker Drive
Suite 4200
Chicago, IL  60606
Phone:      (312) 697-4590          Fax: (312) 697-4598    Email: vmaruri@hispaniapartners.com

Hopewell Ventures, L.P.
Craig Overmyer, Contact
20 North Wacker Drive, Suite 2200
Chicago, IL  60606
Phone:      (312) 357-9600          Fax:(312) 357-9620      Email:
            overmyer@hopewellventures.com

 LaSalle Capital Group, L.P.
Andrew Shackelford, CFO
Three First National Plaza, Suite 5710
Chicago, IL  60602

Phone: (312) 236-7041 Fax:(312) 236-0720 Email: ashackelford@lasallecapitalgroup.com

Prairie Capital II, L.P.
C. Bryan Daniels, Contact
191 N. Wacker Drive, Suite 800
Chicago, IL 60606
Phone: (312) 360-1133 Fax:(312) 360-1193 Email: hlane@prairie-capital.com

Prism Mezzanine Fund SBIC, L.P.
Robert Finkel, Contact
444 N. Michigan Avenue, Suite 1910
Chicago, IL 60611
Phone: (312) 464-7900 Fax:(312) 464-7915 Email: BL@prismfund.com
SvoCo, L.P.
John Svoboda, Michelle Collins, Contacts
1 North Franklin Street, Suite 1500
Chicago, IL 60606
Phone: (312) 267-8750 Fax:(312) 759-7855 Email: jas@svoco.com

Valor Equity Partners, L.P.
Antonio Gracias, Contact
200 S. Michigan Avenue, Suite 1020
Chicago, IL 60604
Phone: (312) 683-1900 Fax:(312) 683-1881 Email: jshulkin@valorep.com

Vogen Funding, L.P.
Jeffery S. Pfeffer, Contact
10 S. Wacker Drive, Suite 1840
Chicago, IL 60606
Phone: (312) 629-2878 Fax:(312) 629-2874 Email: jspfeffer@capxpartners.com

## Indiana
Eugene L. Cavanaugh, Jr., Vice President
P.O. Box 1602
South Bend, IN 46634
Phone: (574)235-2180 Fax:(574) 235-2227 Email: cavanaugh@1stsource.com

Cambridge Ventures, LP
Ms. Jean Wojtowicz, President
4181 East 96th Street, Suite 200
Indianapolis, IN 46240
Phone: (317)814-6192 Fax:(317) 844-9815 Email:
jwojtowicz@cambridgecapitalmgmt.com

Centerfield Capital Partners, L.P.
D. Scott Lutzke, Contact
3030 Market Tower
10 West Market Street
Indianapolis, IN 46204

Phone:     (317) 237-2323       Fax:(317) 237-2325   Email:
SCOTT@centerfieldcapital.com

## Iowa

AAVIN Equity Partners I, L.P.
James D. Thorpe, Contact
118 Third Avenue, SE, Suite 630
Cedar Rapids, IA  52401
Phone:     (319) 247-1072       Fax:(319) 363-9519   Email:     jthorp@aavin.com

Lewis & Clark Private Equities, L.P.
David R. Schroder, Contact
101 Second Street, SE, Suite 800
Cedar Rapids, IA  52401
Phone:     (319)363-8249        Fax:(319) 363-9683   Email:     mbenge@investam.com

North Dakota SBIC, L.P.
David R. Schroder, Manager
101 Second Street SE, Suite 800
Cedar Rapids, IA  52401
Phone:     (701) 298-0003       Fax:(701) 293-7819   Email:     mbenge@investam.com

## Kansas

Kansas Venture Capital, Inc.
Marshall D. Parker
Pinnacle Corporate Centre I, Suite 250
11300 Tomahawk Creek Parkway
Leawood, KS  66211
Phone:     (913) 262-7117       Fax:(913) 262-3509   Email:     mparker@kvci.com

MidStates Capital, L.P.
Timothy J. Keeble, Contact
7300 West 110th Street, 7th Floor
Overland Park, KS  66210
Phone:     (913) 962-9007       Fax:(913) 962-0699   Email:     timk@midstatescap.com

## Kentucky

Chrysalis Ventures II, L.P.
Lisa K. Aly, Contact
101 South Fifth Street, Suite 1650
Louisville, KY  40202
Phone:     (502) 583-7644       Fax:(502) 853-7648   Email:     Laly@ChrysalisVentures.com

Mountain Ventures, Inc.
L. Ray Moncrief, President
P.O. Box 1738, 362 Old Whitley Road
London, KY  40743
Phone:     (606) 864-5175       Fax:(606) 864-5194   Email:     BMcDaniel@khic.org

## Louisiana

Bank One Equity Investors-BIDCO, Inc.
Thomas J. Adamek, President
c/o Stonehenge Capital Corporation
236 Third Street
Baton Rouge, LA 70801
Phone:    (225) 408-3255    Fax:(225) 408-3090    Email:
         sgwhittington@stonehengecapital.com

Jefferson Capital Partners I, L.P.
William J. Harper, Contact
3501 N. Causeway Boulevard., Suite 420
Metairie, LA 70002
Phone:    (504) 828-2088    Fax:(504) 828-2014
Email:    capital@jeffcap.com; wharper@jeffcap.com

## Maine

Masthead Venture Partners Capital, L.P.
Timothy Agnew, Contact
3 Canal Plaza, Suite 600
Portland, ME 04101
Phone:    (207) 780-0905    Fax:(207) 780-0913    Email:    tim@mvpartners.com

North Atlantic SBIC IV, L.P.
Kimberley A. Niles, CFO
Two City Center, 5th Floor
Portland, ME 04101
Phone:    (207) 772-4470    Fax:(207) 772-3257    Email:
         kniles@northatlanticcapital.com
North Atlantic Venture Fund II, L.P.
David M. Coit, Manager
Two City Center, 5th Floor
Portland, ME 04101
Phone:    (207) 772-4470    Fax:(207) 772-3257    Email:
         kniles@northatlanticcapital.com

## Maryland

Allegiance Capital, L.P.
Gary Dorsch
10706 Beaver Dam Road, Suite 201
Cockeysville, MD 21030
Phone:    (410) 568-1715    Fax:(410) 568-1733    Email:    gdorsch@allcapital.com

Anthem Capital II, L.P.
C. Edward Spiva, Contact
The Mangels Building
1414 Key Highway, Suite 300
Baltimore, MD 21230
Phone:    (410) 625-1510    Fax:(410) 625-1735    Email:    cspiva@anthemcapital.com

Legg Mason SBIC Mezzanine Fund, L.P.
Andrew L. John, Contact
111 South Calvert Street
Suite 1800
Baltimore, MD 21202
Phone:    (443) 573-3700    Fax:(443) 573-3703  Email:    ajohn@cscp.com

Patriot Capital II, L.P.
Chris Royston, Contact
The Latrobe Building
2 East Read Street, Suite 101
Baltimore, MD 21202
Phone:    (443) 573-3010    Fax: (443) 573-3020  Email:    croyston@patriot-capital.com

Security Financial and Investment Corp.
Jim Bonfils, Manager
7720 Wisconsin Avenue, Suite 207
Bethesda, MD 20814
Phone:    (301) 951-4288    Fax:(301) 951-4286  Email:    jamesbonfils@aol.com

Spring Capital Partners II, L.P.
Robert M. Stewart, Contact
The Latrobe Building, 5th Floor
2 East Read Street
Baltimore, MD 21202
Phone:    (410) 685-8000    Fax:(410) 545-0015  Email:    rms@springcap.com

Toucan Capital Fund II, L.P.
Mrs. Linda Powers
7600 Wisconsin Avenue, 7th Floor
Bethesda, MD 20814
Phone:    (240) 497-4060    Fax:(240) 497-4065  Email:    info@toucancapital.com

Walker Investment Fund II SBIC, L.P.
Gina Dubbe, Contact
3060 Washington Road, Suite 200
Glenwood, MD 21738
Phone:    (301) 854-6850    Fax:(301) 854-6235  Email:    gina@walkerventures.com

**Massachusetts**
Ascent Venture Partners II, L.P.
Walter Dick, General Partner
255 State Street, 5th Floor
Boston, MA 02109
Phone:    (617) 720-9400    Fax: (617) 720-9401  Email:    tscanlon@ascentvp.com

Brook Venture Fund IIA, L.P.
Andrew Clapp, Contact
301 Edgewater Place, Suite 425
Wakefield, MA 01880-
Phone: (781) 295-4000 Fax:(781) 295-4007 Email: nm@brookventure.com

Chestnut Venture Partners, L.P.
David D. Croll, President
75 State Street, Suite 2500
Boston, MA 02109
Phone: (617) 345-7220 Fax:(617) 345-7201 Email:
dcroll@mcventurepartners.com

Citizens Ventures, Inc.
Scott Sullivan - VP of Finance
28 State Street, 15th Floor
Boston, MA 02109
Phone: (617) 994-7177 Fax:(617) 725-5630 Email:
SCOTT@CITIZENSCAPITAL.COM

Draper Fisher Jurvetson New England Fund I
Todd Hixon, Contact
One Broadway, 14th Floor
Cambridge, MA 02142
Phone: (617) 758-4213 Fax:(617) 758-4101 Email: todd@dfjne.com

Exeter Capital Partners IV, L.P.
Keith Fox, Kurt Bergquist, Jeff Weber
One Liberty Square, 12th Floor
Boston, MA 02109
Phone: (617) 224-0100 Fax:(617)892-4311 Email: Keith.Fox@exeterfunds.com

Gemini Investors III, L.P.
David F. Millet, Contact
20 William Street
Wellesley, MA 02481
Phone: (781) 237-7001 Fax:(781) 237-7233 Email: mkeis@gemini-investors.com

Ironwood Equity Fund LP
18 Tremont St., Suite 1120
Boston, MA 02108
Phone: (617) 723-6747 Fax:(617) 723-6746

Longworth Venture Partners II-A, L.P.
Paul A. Margolis, Contact
1050 Winter Street, Suite 2600
Waltham, MA 02451
Phone: (781) 663-3600 Fax:(781) 663-3619 Email: lawrence@longworth.com

Masthead Venture Partners Capital, L.P.
55 Cambridge Parkway, Suite 103
Cambridge, MA  02142-
Phone:     (617) 621-3000          Fax:(617) 621-3055


North Hill Ventures II, L.P.
Brett Rome, Contact
Ten Post Office Square, Suite 1100
Boston, MA  02109
Phone:     (617) 788-2150          Fax:(617) 788-2152     Email:     brettj.rome@capitalone.com


RockPort Capital Partners, L.P.
Bettina Metais, Contact
160 Federal Street, 18th Floor
Boston, MA  02110
Phone:     (617) 912-1420          Fax:(617) 912-1449     Email:     bmetais@rockportcap.com


Seacoast Capital Partners II, L.P.
Walt Leonard, Contact
55 Ferncroft Road
Danvers, MA  01923
Phone:     (978) 750-1300          Fax:(978) 750-1301     Email:     wleon@seacoastcapital.com


SEED Ventures, L.P.
Thomas Wooters, Contact
80 Dean Street
Taunton, MA  02780
Phone:     (508) 822-1020          Fax:(508) 880-7869     Email:     tom@seedvf.com


Summer Street Capital Fund I, L.P.
Richard Steele
171 Dwight Rd.
Suite 310
Longmeadow, MA  01106-
Phone:     (413) 567-3366          Fax:(413) 567-6556


Ticonderoga SBIC, L.P.
Craig A.T. Jones, Contact
230 Third Avenue
Waltham, MA  02451
Phone:     (781) 416-3400          Fax: (781) 416-9868  Email:     cjones@ticonderogacap.com


Velocity Equity Partners I SBIC, L.P.
David Vogel, Contact
121 High Street
Boston, MA  02110
Phone:     (617) 338-2545          Fax: (617) 261-3864  Email:     jvogel@velocityep.com

Venture Capital Fund of New England IV, L.P
Kevin J. Dougherty, Contact
30 Washington Street
Wellesley Hills, MA 02481
Phone:     (781) 431-8400          Fax: (781) 237-6578   Email:     kdougherty@vcfne.com

Zero Stage Capital V, L.P.
Paul M. Kelley, Manager
265 Franklin Street, 18th Floor
Boston, MA 02110-
Phone:     (617) 876-5355          Fax:(617) 876-1248    Email:     PK@zerostage.com

**Michigan**
Dearborn Capital Corp.   (SSBIC)
Michael Kehres, Asst Treasurer,Secretary
c/o Ford Motor Credit Corporation
The American Road
Dearborn, MI  48121
Phone:     (313) 337-8577          Fax:(313) 390-3783    Email:     mkehres@ford.com

EDF Ventures II, L.P.
Mary Campbell, Contact
425 North Main Street
Ann Arbor, MI  48104-1147
Phone:     (734) 663-3213          Fax:(734) 663-7358    Email:     fingerle@edfvc.com

North Coast Technology Investor, L.P.
Hugo E. Braun III, Lindsay D. Aspegren
206 S. Fifth Avenue Suite 550
Ann Arbor, MI  48104-0648
Phone:     (734) 662-7667          Fax: (734) 662-6261   Email:     hugo@northcoastvc.com

**Minnesota**
AAVIN Equity Partners I, L.P.
Daryl Erdman
2500 Rand Tower
Minneapolis, MN  55402
Phone:     (602) 375-9966          Fax: (319) 363-9519

Affinity Ventures III, L.P.
Robin M. Dowdle, Contact
901 Marquette Avenue, Suite 2820
Minneapolis, MN  55402
Phone:     (612) 252-9897          Fax:(612) 252-9911    Email:     rdowdle@affinitycapital.net

Agio Capital Partners I, L.P.
Kenneth F. Gudorf, President & CEO
5050 Lincoln Drive, Suite 420
Edina, MN  55436

Phone: (952) 938-1628    Fax:(952)933-6066    Email:    Ken@Agio-Capital.com

Bayview Capital Partners, L.P.
Cary Musech, Manager
301 Carlson Parkway, Suite 325
Minnetonka, MN 55305
Phone: (952) 345-2030    Fax:(952) 345-2001    Email:
cmusech@tonkabayequity.com

Convergent Capital Partners I, L.P.
John Mason, Keith Bares
505 N. Highway 169
Suite 245
Minneapolis, MN 55441-
Phone: (763) 432-4081    Fax:(763) 432-4085    Email:    kbares@cvcap.com

GMB Mezzanine Capital, L.P.
Barry Lindquist, Contact
50 South Sixth Street, Suite 1460
Minneapolis, MN 55402
Phone: (612) 243-4404    Fax:(612) 243-4446    Email:    blindquist@gmbmezz.com

Marquette Capital Fund I, L.P.
Thomas Jenkins, Contact
60 South Sixth Street, Suite 3510
Minneapolis, MN 55402
Phone: (612) 661-3990    Fax:(612) 661-3999    Email:    tom.jenkins@marquette.com

Medallion Capital, Inc.
Paul Meyering, President
3000 W. County Road 42, Suite 301
Burnsville, MN 55337-4827
Phone: (952) 831-2025    Fax:(952) 831-2945    Email:
mvannelli@medallioncapital.com

Milestone Growth Fund, Inc.
Richard Venegar, President and CEO
527 Marquette Avenue, Suite 1915
Minneapolis, MN 55402-
Phone: (612) 338-0090    Fax:(612) 338-1172    Email:
dlindorfer@milestonegrowth.com

**Mississippi**
CapSource 2000 Fund, L.P.
James R. Herndon, Contact
795 Woodlands Parkway, Suite 100
Ridgeland, MS 39157
Phone: (601) 899-8980    Fax:(601) 952-1334    Email:    capsources@capsources.com

Sun-Delta Capital Access Center, Inc.   (SSBIC)

Cindy Ayers-Elliott, President
819 Main Street
Greenville, MS 38701
Phone: (662) 335-5291    Fax:(662) 335-5295   Email:    jtaylor@deltadf.org

**Missouri**
American Century Ventures II, L.L.C.
Mark Hyde, Contact
4500 Main Street
Kansas City, MO 64111
Phone: (816) 340-7269    Fax:(816) 340-7125   Email:
            mark_hyde@americancentury.com

BOME Investors II, L.L.C.
Shelley Whittington, Thomas Adamek
c/o Gateway Capco II, LLC
8000 Maryland Avenue, Suite 330
Saint Louis, MO 63105
Phone: (314) 721-5707    Fax: (314) 721-5135

C3 Capital Partners II, L.P.
Patrick F. Healy, Contact
4520 Main Street, Suite 1600
Kansas City, MO 64111-7700
Phone: (816) 756-2225    Fax:(816) 756-5552   Email:    phealy@C3cap.com

CFB Venture Fund L.P.
Greg L. Gaeddert
1000 Walnut, 18th Floor
Kansas City, MO 64106
Phone: (816) 234-2357    Fax:(816) 234-2952

Eagle Fund I, L.P.
Scott Fesler, Principal
101 S. Hanley Road, Suite 1250
St. Louis, MO 63105
Phone: (314) 727-4555    Fax:(314) 727-8829   Email:    bmg@bushodonnell.com

Eagle Fund II, L.P.
Scott Fesler, Principal
101 S. Hanley Road, Suite 1250
St. Louis, MO 63105
Phone: (314) 727-4555    Fax:(314) 727-8829   Email:    sdf@bushodonnell.com

RiverVest Venture Fund I, L.P.
Thomas C. Melzer, Contact
7733 Forsyth Boulevard, Suite 1650
Saint Louis, MO 63105
Phone: (314) 726-6700    Fax:(314) 726-6715   Email:    mslavich@rivervest.com

UMB Capital Corporation, Inc.
Christian P. Roth, Manager
1010 Grand Boulevard
Mail Stop 1020204
Kansas City, MO 64106-
Phone: (816) 860-4871　　Fax:(816) 860-7143　Email:　christian.roth@umb.com

### Montana
Glacier Venture Fund Limited Partnership
Jon Marchi, Contact
40 West 14th Street, Suite 4B
Helena, MT 59624
Phone: (406) 443-2160　　Fax:(406) 443-2161　Email:　jonmarchi@marchiangus.com

### Nebraska
No companies listed.

### Nevada
Atalanta Investment Company, Inc.
L. Mark Newman, Chairman of the Board
601 Fairview Boulevard
P.O. Box 7718
Incline Village, NV 89452
Phone: (775) 833-1836　　Fax: (775) 833-1890　Email:　mark@marknewman.net

### New Hampshire
MB Growth Partners II, L.P.
Jeffrey M. Pollock, Contact
66 Hanover Street
Manchester, NH 03101
Phone: (603) 623-5500　　Fax: (603) 623-3972　Email:
　　　　　jmpollock@merchantbanc.com

MerchantBanc Venture Partners, L.P.
Jeffrey M. Pollock
66 Hanover Street
Suite 303
Manchester, NH 03101
Phone: (603) 623-5500　　Fax: (603) 623-3972　Email:　jrgill@merchantbanc.com

### New Jersey
Alliance Mezzanine Investors, L.P.
Robert Eberhardt, Douglas Smith
96 Pompton Road
Verona, NJ 07044
Phone: (973) 239-8900　　Fax: (973) 239-8909　Email:　rwe@mezcap.com

Contemporary Healthcare Fund I, LP
Eric Smith, Contact
1040 Broad Street, Suite 3B

Shrewsbury, NJ 07702
Phone:    (732) 578-0533    Fax:(732) 578-0501    Email:
    esmith@contemporarycapital.com

DFW Capital Partners, L.P.
Donald F. DeMuth, Manager
Glenpointe Centre East, 5th Floor
300 Frank W. Burr Boulevard
Teaneck, NJ 07666
Phone:    (201) 836-2233    Fax:(201) 836-5666    Email:
    DFDemuth@DFWCapital.com

Edison Fund V, L.P.
Ross Martinson, Contact
1009 Lenox Drive, #4
Lawrenceville, NJ 08648
Phone:    (609) 873-9202    Fax:(609) 896-0066    Email:    gayle@edisonventure.com

Hanam Capital Corp.
Robert Schairer, President
605 Broad Avenue, Suite 202
Ridgefield,, NJ 07657-
Phone:    (201) 943-4400    Fax:(201) 943-4406    Email:    hanam@aol.com

MidMark Capital II, L.P.
Wayne L. Clevenger, Contact
177 Madison Avenue
Morristown, NJ 07960
Phone:    (973) 971-9960    Fax:(973) 971-9963    Email:
    mfinlay@midmarkcapital.com

NJTC Venture Fund SBIC, L.P.
4 Becker Farm Road
Roseland, NJ 07068
Phone:    (973) 994-0606    Fax:(973) 992-6336

Navigator Growth Partners, L.P.
Bernard B. Markey, Contact
P.O. Box 159
Summit, NJ 07902
Phone:    (908) 273-7733    Fax:(908) 273-5566    Email:
    bbmarkey@navigatorequity.com

Sycamore Venture Capital, L.P.
John Whitman
845 Alexander Road
Princeton, NJ 08540
Phone:    (609) 759-8888    Fax:(609) 759-8900    Email:
    dlichtenstein@sycamorevc.com

Tappan Zee Capital Corporation
Jeffrey Birnberg, President
25 Whitney Road
Mahwah, NJ 07430
Phone:      (201) 560-1180         Fax: (201) 560-1158   Email:       jeff@BirnbergGroup.com

University Ventures, Inc.   (SSBIC)
David M. Scheck - Chairman
c/o New Jersey Community Capital
16-18 West Lafayette Street
Trenton, NJ 08608
Phone:      (609) 989-7766         Fax: (609) 393-9401   Email:       dscheck@njclf.com

Ziegler Healthcare Fund I, L.P.
Douglas Korey, Contact
Executive Center #2, Third Floor
1040 Broad Street
Shrewsbury, NJ 07702
Phone:      (732) 578-0533         Fax:(732) 578-0501    Email:
            esmith@contemporarycapital.com

Zon Capital Partners, L.P.
William D. Bridgers, Contact
5 Vaughn Drive, Suite 302
Princeton, NJ 08540
Phone:      (609) 452-1653    Fax:         (609) 452-1693       Email:
            valbruder@zoncapital.com

**New Mexico**
No companies listed.

**New York**
ABN AMRO Capital (USA) Inc.
Mark Burstein, VP & Secretary
55 E. 52nd Street
10th Floor
New York, NY 10055
Phone:      (312) 904-9526         Fax:(312) 904-6684    Email:       aamir.khan@abnamro.com

Accretive Investors SBIC, L.P.
J. Michael Cline, Contact
51 Madison Avenue, 31st Floor
New York, NY 10010
Phone:      (646) 282-1920         Fax:(646) 282-3138    Email: MSlodowitz@accretivellc.com

ACI Capital America Fund, L.P.
Kevin Penn, Thomas Israel, Jim Mattutat
12 East 49th Street, 27th Floor
New York, NY 10017
Phone:      (212) 634-3333         Fax:(212) 634-3330    Email:       jemattutat@acicapital.com

AEA Investors Small Business Fund LP
John F. Cozzi, Contact
55 East 52nd Street, 35th Floor
New York, NY 10055
Phone:    (212) 702-0504        Fax:(212) 702-0550    Email:    jcozzi@aeainvestors.com

Argentum Capital Partners II, L.P.
Daniel Raynor, Chairman
60 Madison Avenue, Suite 701
New York, NY 10110
Phone:    (212) 949-6262        Fax:(212) 949-8294    Email:
          sdberman@argentumgroup.com

BMO Capital Markets Equity Investments (US)
Peter Hurwitz - Managing Director
3 Times Square
28th. Floor
New York, NY 10036
Phone:    (212) 605-1687        Fax:(212) 765-8000    Email:    helen.schubbe@bmonb.com

BNY Capital Partners, L.P.
Stratton Heath, Paul Echausse
200 Park Avenue
55th Floor
New York, NY 10166
Phone:    (212) 922-8195        Fax:(212) 922-6585    Email:    pechausse@bankofny.com

BOCNY, LLC
W. Stephen Keller
C/O Stonehenge Capital Corporation
152 West 57th Street, 20th Floor
New York, NY 10019
Phone:    (212) 944-2542        Fax:(212) 656-1344    Email:
          adkocen@stonehengecapital.com

Brookside Pecks Capital Partners, L.P.
Ray Weldon
405 Park Avenue, 12th Floor
New York, NY 10022
Phone:    (212) 935-6090        Fax:(212) 759-4831

Cephas Capital Partners L.P.
Clint Campbell, Jeff Holmes, Mgrs.
57 Monroe Avenue, Suite D
Pittsford, NY 14534
Phone:    (585) 383-1610        Fax:(585) 383-1613    Email: ccampbell@cephascapital.com

CIBC WMV Inc.
David Shotland, Managing Director

425 Lexington Avenue, 9th Floor
New York, NY  10017
Phone:     (212) 856-4072        Fax:(212) 697-1544     Email:
            David.Shotland@US.CIBC.com

Citicorp Venture Capital, Ltd.
William Comfort, Chairman
399 Park Avenue, 14th Floor/Zone 4
New York, NY  10043
Phone:     (212) 559-1132        Fax:(212) 793-6164     Email:     meghan.fogarty@citi.com

Critical Capital Growth Fund, L.P.
Steven Sands Mgr; C. Robinson
90 Park Avenue, 31st Floor
New York, NY  10016
Phone:     (212) 697-5200        Fax:(212) 697-8035     Email:     crobinson@laidlawltd.com

DeltaPoint Capital III, L.P.
David H. Waterman, Managing Director
45 East Avenue, 6th Floor
Rochester, NY  14604
Phone:     (585) 454-6990        Fax:(585) 454-3204     Email:
            dwaterman@deltapointcapital.com

East Coast Venture Capital, Inc.   (SSBIC)
Fredrick Schulman, President
30 East 29th Street, Suite 204
New York, NY  10016
Phone:     (212) 686-1515        Fax:(212) 686-1131     Email:     fstart@aol.com

Easton Hunt Capital Partners, L.P.
John H. Friedman, Contact
767 Third Avenue, 7th Floor
New York, NY  10017
Phone:     (212) 702-0950        Fax:(212) 702-0952     Email:     schneider@eastoncapital.com

Elk Associates Funding Corporation
Gary C. Granoff, President
747 Third Avenue
New York, NY  10017
Phone:     (212) 421-2111        Fax:(212) 759-3338     Email:     lforlenza@elkassociates.com

Emigrant Capital Corporation
Kenneth L. Walters Jr.
6 East 43rd Street
8th Floor
New York, NY  10017
Phone:     (212) 850-4470        Fax:(212) 850-3470     Email:     WaltersK@emigrant.com

Empire State Capital Corporation   (SSBIC)
Mitzi Wu, Vice President
170 Broadway, Suite 404
New York, NY  10038
Phone:      (212) 513-1799          Fax:(212) 513-1892   Email:      ESC5131799@aol.com


Eos Partners SBIC II, L.P.
Steven Friedman & Brian Young, Manager
320 Park Avenue, 22nd Floor
New York, NY  10022
Phone:      (212) 832-5800          Fax:(212) 832-5805   Email:      bbernstein@eospartners.com

Falcon Private Equity, L.P.
Gregga Baxter, Matthew Snyder, Contacts
330 Madison Avenue - 37th Floor
New York, NY  10017-4627
Phone:      (212) 922-2333          Fax:(212) 922-2351   Email:
            gregga.baxter@saudibank.com

Flushing Capital Corporation   (SSBIC)
Tetsuro Takada, President
113-19 14th Road
College Point, NY  11356
Phone:      (718) 886-5866          Fax:(718) 321-2934   Email:      flushingcapital@nyc.rr.com

Founders Equity SBIC I, L.P.
John D. White, Jr., Contact
711 Fifth Avenue, 5th Floor
New York, NY  10022
Phone:      (212) 829-0900          Fax:(212) 829-0901   Email:      darton@fequity.com

Freshstart Venture Capital Corporation
Alvin Murstein, President
437 Madison Avenue
New York, NY  10022
Phone:      (212) 328-2110          Fax:(212) 328-2125   Email:      mrusso@medallion.com

Fundex Capital Corp.
Larry Linksman, President
50 Main Street, Suite 1000
White Plains, NY  10606
Phone:      (212) 884-9360          Fax:(212) 884-9346   Email:
            L.Linksman@fundexcapital.com
Gefus SBIC, L.P.
William J. Beckett
375 Park Avenue, Suite 2401
New York, NY  10152
Phone:      (212) 308-1111          Fax:(212) 308-1182   Email:      wbeckett@gefinorusa.com

High Peaks Ventures, L.P.
Russell Howard, Contact
10 Second Street
Troy, NY 12180
Phone:     (518) 720-3090      Fax:(518) 720-3091    Email:    russ@highpeaksventures.com

Hudson Venture Partners II, L.P.
Dr. Lawrence A. Howard, Contact
535 Fifth Avenue, 14th Floor
New York, NY 10017
Phone:     (212) 644-9797      Fax: (212) 644-7430   Email:    jtruehart@hudsonptr.com

Ibero American Investors Corp.
Emilio Serrano, President
104 Scio Street
Rochester, NY 14604
Phone:     (585) 262-3440      Fax: (585) 262-3441   Email:    iberoinv@rochester.rr.com

ING Furman Selz Investments
Brian Friedman, Manager
520 Madison Avenue
8th Floor
New York, NY 10022
Phone:     (212) 284-1708      Fax:(212) 284-1717    Email:    mluxenberg@fsprivate.com

KBL Healthcare, L.P.
Marlene Krauss, Michael Kaswan
380 Lexington Avenue, 31st Floor
New York, NY 10022
Phone:     (212) 319-5555      Fax:(212) 319-5591    Email:    ss@kblvc.com

Kinderhook Capital SBIC Fund I, L.P.
Robert Michalik, Contact
888 7th Avenue
16th Floor
New York, NY 10106
Phone:     (212) 201-6780      Fax:(212) 201-6790    Email:
           rmichalik@kinderhookcapital.com

L Capital Partners SBIC, LP
Oded Weiss, Contact
10 East 53rd Street, 37th Floor
New York, NY 10022
Phone:     (212) 675-7755      Fax:(212) 206-9156    Email:    oded@lcapitalpartners.com

LEG Partners SBIC, L.P.
Lawrence Golub, Manager
551 Madison Avenue, 6th Floor
New York, NY 10022
Phone:     (212) 750-6060      Fax:(212) 750-5505    Email:    rzomback@golubcapital.com

M & T Capital Corp.
Tom Scanlon, President
One Fountain Plaza
3rd Floor
Buffalo, NY 14203
Phone:     (716) 848-3800     Fax:(716) 848-3150   Email:     tscanlon1@mandtbank.com

Medallion Funding Corporation
Alvin Murstein, President
437 Madison Avenue
New York, NY 10022
Phone:     (212) 328-2110     Fax:(212) 328-2125   Email:     nsarna@medallion.com

Merchants Capital Partners, L.P.
Jake Wessner
1120 Avenue of the Americas - 4th Floor
New York, NY 10036
Phone:     (212) 626-6832     Fax:(212) 626-6833

Mercury Capital, L.P.
David W. Elenowitz, Contact
590 Madison Avenue
30th Floor
New York, NY 10022
Phone:     (212) 838-0888     Fax: (212) 759-3897   Email:     ele@mercurycapitalinc.com

NBT Capital Corporation
Daryl Forsythe & Joe Minor, Managers
52 South Broad Street
Norwich, NY 13815
Phone:     (607) 337-6810     Fax: (607) 336-8730   Email:     rpowell@nbtbank.com

Praesidian Capital Investors, LP
Jason D. Drattell, Contact
419 Park Avenue South
New York, NY 10016
Phone:     (212) 520-2600     Fax:(212) 520-2601   Email:     jdrattell@praesidian.com

Radius Venture Partners II, L.P.
Daniel C. Lubin, Contact
400 Madison Avenue, 8th Floor
New York, NY 10017
Phone:     (212) 897-7784     Fax: (212) 397-2656   Email:     dlubin@radiusventures.com

Rand Capital SBIC, L.P.
Allen F. Grum, Jr., Contact
2200 Rand Buidling
Buffalo, NY 14203
Phone:     (716) 853-0802     Fax: (716) 854-8480   Email:     dpenberthy@randcapital.com

Rock Maple Ventures, L.P.
David W. Freelove, Contact
711 Fifth Avenue, 5th Floor
New York, NY 10022
Phone:     (212) 813-2720        Fax: (212) 813-2730   Email:
                dfreelove@rockmapleventures.com
Scorpion Capital Partners, L.P.
Kevin R. McCarthy, Contact
245 Fifth Avenue, 25th Floor
New York, NY 10016
Phone:     (212) 213-9190        Fax: (212) 213-9607   Email:
                Kmccarthy@scorpioncap.com

Summer Street Capital Fund I, L.P.
Brian D'Amico
70 West Chippewa Street
Suite 500
Buffalo, NY 14202
Phone:     (716) 566-2900        Fax: (716) 566-2910   Email:
                bdamico@summerstreetcapital.com

Sunrise Equity Partners, L.P.
Marilyn S. Adler, Contact
641 Lexington Avenue, 25th Floor
New York, NY 10022
Phone:     (212) 421-1616        Fax:(212) 750-7277   Email:        marilyna@sunrisecorp.com

The 1818 SBIC Fund, L.P.
Richard J. Ragoza, Contact
c/o Brown Brothers Harriman & Co.
140 Broadway, 2nd Floor
New York, NY 10005
Phone:     (212) 493-7910        Fax:(212) 493-8832   Email:        rick.ragoza@bbh.com

Triad Capital Corp. of New York   (SSBIC)
Oscar Figueroa - Investment Manager
305 Seventh Avenue, 20th Floor
New York, NY 10001
Phone:     (212)243-7360        Fax: (212) 243-7647      Email: ofigueroa@bcfcapital.com

Trumpet SBIC Partners, L.P.
Marc Utay, Contact
110 East 59th Street, Suite 2100
New York, NY 10022
Phone:     (212) 821-0177        Fax: (212) 371-7597   Email:        mutay@clarion-capital.com

Westbury Equity Partners SBIC, L.P.
Richard P. Sicoli, Contact
100 Motor Parkway, Suite 165
Hauppauge, NY 11788
Phone: (631) 231-4121 Fax: (631) 231-8121 Email:
rsicoli@westburypartners.com

**North Carolina**
BA Capital Company, L.P.
J. Travis Hain, Managing Member
100 North Tryon Street, 25th Floor
NCI-007-25-02
Charlotte, NC 28255
Phone: (704) 386-1792 Fax: (704) 386-6432 Email:
ed.a.balogh@bankofamerica.com

Banc of America Capital Investors SBIC, L.P
J. Travis Hain, Managing Member
100 North Tryon Street, 25th Floor
NC1-007-25-02
Charlotte, NC 28255
Phone: (704) 386-1792 Fax:(704) 386-6432 Email:
ed.a.balogh@bankofamerica.com

BancBoston Ventures, Incorporated
Erick C. Christensen
Bank of America Corporate Center
Mail Code: NC1-007-22-32
Charlotte, NC 28255-0001
Phone: (704) 683-5741 Fax:(704) 388-2746 Email:
erick.c.christensen@bankofamerica.com

BB&T Capital Partners II, LLC
David Townsend, Contact
101 N. Cherry Street, Suite 700
Winston-Salem, NC 27101-4019
Phone: (336) 733-0355 Fax:(336) 733-0349 Email: dgtownsend@bbandt.com

BB&T Capital Partners/Windsor Mezzanine Fun
David Townsend
101 N. Cherry Street, Suite 700
Winston-Salem, NC 27101-4019
Phone: (336) 733-0355 Fax:(336) 733-0349 Email: Cnjones@bbandt.com

CapitalSouth Partners Fund I, L.P.
Jack McGlinn
2530 Meridian Parkway, Suite 200
Research Triangle Park
Durham, NC 27713
Phone:     (919) 806-4590          Fax:(866) 801-6581

CapitalSouth Partners Fund II, L.P.
Joseph B. Alala, Contact
1011 East Morehead Street, Suite 150
Charlotte, NC 28204
Phone:     (704) 376-5502          Fax:(704) 376-5877     Email:
           jalala@capitalsouthpartners.com

Frontier Fund I, L.P.
Andrew Lender, Contact
1900 South Boulevard, Suite 300
Charlotte, NC 28203
Phone:     (704) 414-2880          Fax:(704) 414-2881     Email:     andrew@frontierfunds.com

North Carolina Economic Opportunities Fund,
H. Dabney Smith, Contact
316 West Edenton Street, Suite 110
Raleigh, NC 27603
Phone:     (919) 256-5007          Fax:(919) 256-5015     Email:     dsmith@dogwoodequity.com

Oberlin Capital, L.P.
Robert Shepley, Manager
4237 Louisburg Road, Suite 105
Raleigh, NC 27604
Phone:     (919) 861-2908          Fax:(919) 861-2901     Email:
           wgupton@greenhawkcapital.com
Plexus Fund I, L.P.
Robert Anders, Jr., Contact
200 Providence Road, Suite 210
Charlotte, NC 28207
Phone:     (704) 927-6246          Fax: (704) 927-6255     Email:     banders@plexuscap.com

Salem Capital Partners II, L.P.
Philip Martin, Contact
112 Cambridge Plaza Drive, Suite 201
Winston-Salem, NC 27114
Phone:     (336) 768-9343          Fax:(336) 768-6471     Email:     pmartin@salemcapital.com

Triangle Mezzanine Fund LLLP
Brent Burgess
3600 Glenwood Avenue, Suite 104
Raleigh, NC 27612
Phone:     (919) 719-4788          Fax:(919) 719-4777     Email:     bburgess@tcap.com

## North Dakota

North Dakota SBIC, L.P.
John G. Cosgriff, Manager
51 Broadway, Suite 400
Fargo, ND 58102
Phone:     (701) 298-0003     Fax: (701) 293-7819

## Ohio

ACP-I, L.P.
Lynn Carpenter, Contact
10 1/2 East Washington Street
Chagrin Falls, OH 44022
Phone:     (440) 247-2800     Fax:(440) 247-3060   Email:   lwc@sfspartners.com

Capvest Ventures, L.P.
Jakki Haussler, Contact
14 S. High Street
P.O. Box 673
New Albany, OH 43054
Phone:     (513) 721-8831     Fax:(513) 639-3072   Email:   jhaussler@capvestvc.com

Capvest Ventures, L.P.
One West 4th Street
Suite 415
Cincinnati, OH 45202
Phone:     (513) 721-8831     Fax:(513) 639-3072

Clarion Capital Corp.
Tom Niehaus, CFO
3690 Orange Place, Suite 400
Beachwood, OH 44122
Phone:     (216) 896-1260     Fax:(216) 896-1261   Email:   karena@clariongrp.com

Enterprise Ohio Investment Company   (SSBIC)
Janet White, Manager
8 North Main Street
Dayton, OH 45402
Phone:     (937) 226-0457     Fax:(937) 222-7035   Email:   jwhite@citywidedev.com

Key Equity Capital Corporation
David Given, President
127 Public Square, 51st Floor
Cleveland, OH 44114
Phone:     (216) 535-4711     Fax:(216) 689-3204   Email:   lroot@bluepointcapital.com

National City Equity Partners, Inc.
William H. Schecter, President & G.M.
1965 East Sixth Street, Suite 1010
Cleveland, OH 44114

Phone:     (216) 222-2491     Fax:(216) 222-9965     Email:     Sharon.breznak@ncepi.com

Peppertree Capital Fund, L.P.
Howard Mandel, Contact
3550 Lander Road, Suite 300
Pepper Pike, OH  44124
Phone:     (216) 514-4949     Fax:(216) 514-4959     Email:
            hmandel@peppertreefund.com

River Cities Capital Fund L.P.
R. Glen Mayfield, Manager
221 East Fourth Street, Suite 2400
Cincinnati, OH  45202
Phone:     (513) 621-9700     Fax:(513) 579-8939     Email:     trobinson@rccf.com

River Cities SBIC III, L.P.
Edwin T. Robinson, Contact
221 East Fourth Street, Suite 2400
Cincinnati, OH  45202
Phone:     (513) 621-9700     Fax:(513) 579-8939     Email:     trobinson@rccf.com

Stonehenge Opportunity Fund II, L.P.
Richard Martinko, Principal
526 Superior Ave., Suite 1140
Cleveland, OH  44114
Phone:     (216) 696-2650     Fax:(216) 696-8326

Stonehenge Opportunity Fund II, L.P.
B. Michael Affinito, Contact
191 West Nationwide Blvd., Suite 600
Columbus, OH  43215
Phone:     (614) 246-2500     Fax:(614) 246-2582     Email:
            bmaffinito@stonehengepartners.com

Triathlon Medical Ventures Fund LP
Suzette L. Dutch, Contact
250 East 5th Street 1100 Chiquita Center
Cincinnati, OH  45202
Phone:     (513) 723-2618     Fax:(513) 723-2615     Email:     sdutch@tmvp.com


Walnut Investment Partners, L.P.
James Gould, Managing Partner
312 Walnut Street, Suite 1151
Cincinnati, OH  45202
Phone:     (513) 651-3300     Fax:(513) 651-1084     Email:
            bonnie.taylor@thewalnutgroup.com

Walnut Private Equity Fund, L.P.
R. Scott Barnes, Contact

312 Walnut Street, Suite 1151
Cincinnati, OH 45202
Phone: (513) 651-3300      Fax:(513) 651-1084    Email:
        bonnie.taylor@thewalnutgroup.com

## Oklahoma
Council Oak Investment Corporation
William O. Johnstone - Manager
101 North Broadway, Suite 400
Oklahoma City, OK 73102
Phone: (405) 218-4696      Fax:(405) 218-4672    Email:    woj@bancfirst.com

First United Venture Capital Corporation
Greg Massey - Vice President
P.O. Box 130
Durant, OK 74702-0130
Phone: (918) 227-5267      Fax:(918) 227-5234    Email:    bertd@firstunitedbank.com

## Oregon
Northern Pacific Capital Corporation
Joseph P. Tennant, President
937 S.W. 14th Street, Suite 200
Mail: P.O. Box 1658
Portland, OR 97207
Phone: (503) 241-1255      Fax:(503) 299-6653    Email:    TRCT@comcast.net

Tamarack Mezzanine Partners, L.P.
John Woolley, Contact
3689 Carman Drive., Suite 200
Lake Oswego, OR 97035-
Phone: (503) 517-8939      Fax:(503) 517-8938    Email:    john@tamarackcapital.com

## Pennsylvania
Argosy Investment Partners II, L.P.
Kirk B. Griswold, Manager
950 West Valley Road, Suite 2900
Wayne, PA 19087
Phone: (610) 971-9685      Fax:(610) 964-9524    Email:    kirk@argosycapital.com

Argosy Investment Partners, L.P.
John P. Kirwin, Manager
950 West Valley Road, Suite 2900
Wayne, PA 19087
Phone: (610) 971-9685      Fax:(610) 964-9524    Email:    kirk@argosycapital.com

CIP Capital L.P.
Ed Carey, Manager
1200 Liberty Ridge Drive, Suite 300
Wayne, PA 19087
Phone:     (610) 964-7875          Fax:(610) 964-8136    Email:    ecarey@cipcapital.com

GIV Venture Partners, L.P.
William Melton
Suites@University Technology Park II
1350 Edgmont Avenue, Suite 2550
Chester, PA 19013
Phone:     (302) 239-9302          Fax:(302) 239-9322    Email:    bill@givinc.com

Lancet Capital Health Ventures, L.P.
William Golden, Manager
100 Technology Drive, Suite 200
Pittsburgh, PA 15219
Phone:     (412) 471-7101          Fax:(412) 770-1342    Email:    golden@lancetcapital.com

Liberty Ventures II, L.P.
Thomas R. Morse, Contact Ext. 24
Two Commerce Square
2001 Market Street, Suite 3820
Philadelphia, PA 19103
Phone:     (267) 861-5692          Fax:(267) 861-5696    Email:    mhahn@libertyvp.com

Meridian Venture Partners II, L.P.
Robert E. Brown, Jr., Contact
201 King of Prussia Road, Suite 240
Radnor, PA 19087
Phone:     (610) 254-2999          Fax:(610) 254-2996    Email:    rbroderick@meridian-
venture.com

Merion Investment Partners, L.P.
William M. Means, Contact
700 South Henderson Road, Suite 210
King of Prussia, PA 19406
Phone:     (610) 992-5881          Fax:(610) 945-1654    Email:
        ghughes@merionpartners.com

NewSpring Mezzanine Capital, L.P.
Marc Lederman, Contact
Radnor Financial Center
555 E. Lancaster Ave, Suite 520
Radnor, PA 19087
Phone:     (610) 567-2380          Fax:(610) 567-2388    Email:
        marc@newspringventures.com

Select Capital Ventures I, L.P.
Michael E. Salerno, Contact
4718 Old Gettysburg Road, Suite 405
Mechanicsburg, PA 17055
Phone:     (717) 972-1304          Fax:(717) 972-1050    Email:     dhellyer@samtrust.net

## Rhode Island
BCA Mezzanine Fund, L.P.
Gregory F. Mulligan, Managing Member
One Turks Head Place, Suite 1492
Providence, RI 02903
Phone:     (401) 228-3834          Fax:(401) 228-3835    Email:     Greg@baycapllc.com

Domestic Capital Corp.
Nathaniel B. Baker, President
815 Reservoir Avenue
Cranston, RI 02910
Phone:     (401) 946-3310          Fax: (401) 943-6708   Email:     gdegioia@Domestic.com

Fleet Venture Resources, Inc.
Ed Resnick, Sr. Portfolio Administrator
50 Kennedy Plaza, 12th Floor
Providence, RI 02903
Phone:     (401) 278-6809          Fax: (401) 278-6387

## South Carolina
CF Investment Company
William S. Hummers III, Manager
104 South Main Street, Poinsett Plaza
Greenville, SC 29601
Phone:     (864) 255-4919          Fax:(864) 239-6423    Email:
           kevin.mast@thesouthgroup.com

## South Dakota
Bluestem Capital Partners III, L.P.
Sandy Horst, Contact
122 S. Phillips Avenue, Suite 300
Sioux Falls, SD 57104
Phone:     (605) 331-0091          Fax:(605) 334-1218    Email:     shorst@bluestemcapital.com

## Tennessee
FCA Venture Partners III SBIC, L.P.
Stuart C. McWhorter, Contact
113 Seaboard Lane, Suite A-250
Franklin, TN 37067
Phone:     (615) 435-2985          Fax:(615) 963-3847    Email:
           allenn@claytonassociates.com

Morgan Keegan Mezzanine Fund, L.P.
William J. Nutter, Contact
30 Burton Hills Blvd., Suite 500
Nashville, TN 37215
Phone: (615) 665-3636 Fax:(615) 665-3670 Email:
bill.nutter@morgankeegan.com

Petra Growth Fund, L.P.
Michael Blackburn, Robert A. Smith
3825 Bedford Avenue, Suite 101
Nashville, TN 37215
Phone: (615) 313-5999 Fax:(615) 313-5990 Email: ras@petracapital.com

Pharos Capital Partners II, L.P.
Kneeland Youngblood, Contact
1 Burton Hills Boulevard, Suite 180
Nashville, TN 37215
Phone: (615) 234-5522 Fax:(615) 263-0234 Email: jgoldberg@pharosfunds.com

Valley Capital Corp. (SSBIC)
Lamar J. Partridge, President
535 Chestnut Street, Suite 368
P.O. Box 11086
Chattanooga, TN 37402
Phone: (423) 265-1557 Fax: (423) 265-1588 Email: ValleyCapital@aol.com

**Texas**
Alliance Enterprise Corporation
Donald R. Lawhorne, President
2435 N. Central Expressway, Suite 200
Richardson, TX 75080
Phone: (972) 991-1597 Fax: (972) 991-4770 Email: sba@pacesettercapital.com

BA Capital Company, L.P.
Doug Williamson, Sr. Vice President
901 Main Street, 22nd Floor
Dallas, TX 75202
Phone: (214) 508-0900 Fax:(214) 508-0985

Blue Sage Capital, L.P.
Peter Huff, Contact
114 West 7th Street, Suite 820
Austin, TX 78701
Phone: (512) 536-1900 Fax:(512) 236-9215 Email: peter.huff@bluesage.com

Capital Southwest Venture Corp.
Gary Martin, President
12900 Preston Road, Suite 700
Dallas, TX 75230

Phone: (972) 233-8242     Fax:(972) 233-7362    Email: gmartin@capitalsouthwest.com

Catalyst Fund, Ltd. (The)
Richard L. Herrman, Manager
Two Riverway, Suite 1710
Houston, TX 77056
Phone: (713) 623-8133     Fax:(713) 623-0473    Email: rherrman@catalysthall.com

First Capital Group of Texas III, L.P.
Jeffrey P. Blanchard, Contact
750 E. Mulberry, Suite 305
San Antonio, TX 78212
Phone: (210) 736-4233     Fax:(210) 736-5449    Email: jpblanchard@firstcapitalgroup.com

Independent Bankers Capital Fund, L.P.
Barry Conrad, Tom Hoyt, Contacts
1700 Pacific Avenue, Suite 2740
Dallas, TX 75201
Phone: (214) 765-1350     Fax:(214) 765-1360    Email: mtaylor@independentbankerscap.com

Jardine Capital Corp.
Lawrence Wong, President
4610 Riverstone Boulevard
Missouri City, TX 77459-
Phone: (713) 271-7077     Fax:(713) 271-7577    Email: lklwong@yahoo.com

Main Street Capital II, LP
Todd Reppert, Contact
1300 Post Oak Boulevard, Suite 800
Houston, TX 77056
Phone: (713) 350-6005     Fax:(713) 350-6001    Email: treppert@mainstreethouston.com

Main Street Mezzanine Fund, L.P.
Todd A. Reppert, Contact
1300 Post Oak Boulevard, Suite 800
Houston, TX 77056
Phone: (713) 350-6000     Fax:(713) 350-6042    Email: treppert@mainstreethouston.com

MESBIC Ventures, Inc.
Donald R. Lawhorne, President
2435 North Central Expressway, Suite 200
Richardson, TX 75080
Phone: (972) 991-1597     Fax:(972) 991-4770    Email: sba@pacesettercapital.com

North Texas MESBIC, Inc.
Allan Lee, President
4563 W. Walnut Street, Suite 200
Garland, TX 75042-5143
Phone:     (972) 272-0388        Fax:(972) 272-0988   Email:     NTM168@aol.com

PMC Investment Corporation
Andrew S. Rosemore, President
17950 Preston Road, Suite 600
Dallas, TX 75252
Phone:     (972) 349-3200        Fax:(972) 349-3265   Email:     b.berlin@pmctrust.com

Power Equities, Inc.
Donald Lawhorne and Thomas Gerron
2435 North Central Expressway, Suite 200
Richardson, TX 75080
Phone:     (972) 991-1597        Fax:(972) 991-4770   Email:     info@mvhc.com

Red River Ventures I, L.P.
J. Bruce Duty, Contact
6860 N. Dallas Parkway, Suite 200
Plano, TX 75024
Phone:     (972) 265-7946        Fax:(972) 265-7995   Email:     bruce@redriverventures.com

Stratford Equity Partners, L.P.
David Knickel, Manager
200 Crescent Court, 16th Floor
Dallas, TX 75201
Phone:     (214) 740-7370        Fax:(214) 740-7393   Email:     lthompson@hmcapital.com

SunTx Fulcrum Fund II - SBIC, L.P.
Ned N. Fleming, Contact
Two Lincoln Centre
5420 LBJ Freeway, Suite 1000
Dallas, TX 75240
Phone:     (972) 663-8901        Fax:(972) 661-9977   Email:     tkelly@suntx.com

Toronto Dominion Capital (U.S.A.), Inc.
Martha Gariepy, Contact
909 Fannin, Suite 1950
Houston, TX 77010
Fax:       (713) 652-2647                              Email:
           Martha.Gariepy@TDCapital.com

Western Financial Capital Corporation
Andrew S. Rosemore, President
17950 Preston Road, Suite 600
Dallas, TX 75252
Phone:     (972) 349-3200  Fax:(972) 349-3265         Email:     b.berlin@pmctrust.com

## Utah

Peterson Partners III, L.P.
Rick Stratford, Contact
2825 E. Cottonwood Parkway
Suite 400
Salt Lake City, UT 84121
Phone:     (801) 365-0180        Fax:(801) 365-0181     Email:     rick@petersonpartnerslp.com

Utah Ventures III, L.P.
James C. Dreyfous, Contact
2755 E. Cottonwood Parkway, Suite 520
Salt Lake City, UT 84121
Phone:     (801) 365-0262        Fax:(801) 365-0233     Email:     jmckay@uven.com

UTFC Financing Solutions, LLC
Steve Grizzell, Contact
699 East  South Temple, Suite 220
Salt Lake City, UT 84102
Phone:     (801) 741-4215        Fax:(801) 741-4249     Email:     sgrizzell@utfc.org

UTFC Fund II, LLC
Scott Stenberg, Contact
699 East South Temple, Suite 220
Salt Lake City, UT 84102
Phone:     (801) 741-4200        Fax: (801) 741-4249    Email:     scott@utfc.com

vSpring SBIC, L.P.
Dinesh Patel, Contact
2795 E. Cottonwood Parkway, Suite 360
Salt Lake City, UT 84121
Phone:     (801) 942-8999        Fax: (801) 942-1636    Email:     David@vspring.com

Wasatch Venture Corporation
Todd J. Stevens, Secretary
1 South Main Street, 8th Floor
Salt Lake City, UT 84133-
Phone:     (801) 524-8939        Fax:(801) 524-8941     Email:     tstevens@wasatchvc.com

Zions SBIC, L.L.C.
Todd J. Stevens, Contact
One South Main Street, Suite 1660
Salt Lake City, UT 84133
Phone:     (801) 524-8939        Fax: (801) 524-8941    Email:     tstevens@wasatchvc.com

## Vermont

North Atlantic Venture Fund II, L.P.
Gregory B. Peters, Vice President
76 St. Paul Street, Suite 600
Burlington, VT 05401
Phone:     (802) 658-7820        Fax:(802) 658-5757

**Virginia**

BIA Digital Partners SBIC II LP
Lloyd Sams, Contact
15120 Enterprise Court, Suite 200
Chantilly, VA 20151
Phone: (703) 227-9600    Fax:(703) 227-9645    Email:    lsams@bia.com

Development Capital Ventures, L.P.
Wayne S. Foren, Contact
7500 Iron Bar Lane, Suite 209
Gainseville, VA 20155
Phone: (571) 261-9620    Fax:(571) 261-9622    Email:    wnickisch@dccgrowth.com

GIV Venture Partners, L.P.
10790 Parkridge Blvd 300
Reston, VA 20191

Gladstone SSBIC Corporation
George Stelljes, Contact
1521 Westbranch Drive, Suite 200
McLean, VA 22102
Phone: (703) 287-5800    Fax:(703) 287-5801    Email:
chipstellges@gladstonemanagement.com

Solutions Capital I, L.P.
Andrew Jacobson, Contact
1100 Wilson Boulevard, Suite 3000
Arlington, VA 22209
Phone: (703) 247-7527    Fax:(866) 405-1622    Email:    ajacobson@mcgcapital.com

Virginia Capital SBIC, L.P.
Frederick Russell & Tom Deardorff, Mgrs.
1801 Libbie Avenue, Suite 201
Richmond, VA 23226
Phone: (804) 648-4802   Fax:(804) 648-4809    Email:    fred@vacapital.com

Waterside Capital Corporation
Franklin (Lin) P. Earley, CEO
500 East Main Street, Suite 800
Norfolk, VA 23510
Phone: (757) 626-1111   Fax:(757) 626-0114    Email:
         julie.stroh@watersidecapital.com

**Virgin Islands**
**No companies listed**

## Washington

Bancshares Capital, L.P.
John E. Thoresen, Contact
16118 72nd Ave W.
Edmonds, WA  98026
Phone:      (206) 948-1195          Fax:(425) 424-0809    Email:      bancshares_lp@msn.com

Fluke Venture Partners II, L.P.
Kevin C. Gabelein, Contact
11400 SE 6th Street, Suite 230
Bellevue, WA  98004
Phone:      (425) 453-4590          Fax:(425) 453-4675    Email:      gabelein@flukeventures.com

Integra Ventures III, L.P.
Tim T. Black, Contact
300 E. Pine, 2nd Floor
Seattle, WA  98122
Phone:      (206) 832-1990          Fax:(206) 832-1991    Email:      Black@IntegraVentures.net

Northwest Venture Partners III, L.P.
Jean Balek-Miner, Contact
221 North Wall Street, Suite 628
Spokane, WA  99201
Phone:      (509) 747-0728          Fax: (509) 747-0758   Email:      jean@nwva.com

## West Virginia
Mountaineer Capital, L.P.
Patrick A. Bond, Contact
107 Capitol Street, Suite 300
Charleston, WV  25301
Phone:      (304) 347-7521          Fax:(304) 347-0072    Email:      angi@mtncap.com

## Wisconsin
Banc One Stonehenge Capital Fund WI, LLC
Mr. Kent Velde, Manager
3424 N. Shepard Avenue
Milwaukee, WI  53211
Phone:      (414) 906-1702          Fax:(414) 906-1703    Email:      kvelde@att.net

M & I Ventures, L.L.C.
John T. Byrnes, President
411 E. Wisconsin Avenue, Suite 1280
Milwaukee, WI  53202
Phone:      (414) 727-6411          Fax:(414) 727-6410    Email:      worthober@masonwells.com

## Wyoming
**No companies listed**

## Guam
**No companies listed**

**Puerto Rico**

North America Investment Corporation   (SSBIC)
Marcelino Pastrana Torres, President
P.O. Box 191831
San Juan, PR  00919-1831
Phone:     (787) 754-6178          Fax:(787) 754-6181     Email:        namerica.naic@gmail.com

Puerto Rico Entrepreneurs Fund, L.P.
Abdon G. Ruiz, Contact
Union Plaza, Suite 1500
416 Ponce de Leon Avenue
San Juan, PR  00918
Phone:     (787) 620-0062          Fax:(787) 620-0131     Email:
          zmendez@miraderocapital.com

TIP: When seeking capital the best way to get started is to write the company asking for a list of their guidelines for project funding. They will send a detailed list.

# UNDERSTANDING BUSINESS FINANCING

One thing is for sure in business, there is never enough money. You constantly need cash to keep your business running. Money is needed for everything. Under the cash crunch banks have virtually eliminated funding for entrepreneurs and the smaller businesses. That's one reason the use of venture capital companies has exploded over the past ten years. Before contacting a venture capital firm you need to understand the certain terminology in order to properly project your financing needs.

The following is a list of the different stages of businesses used to evaluate financing needs:

Seed Stage - This stage is where the idea is formulated. Here is where the research is conducted to determine whether or not an new idea or product will be well received by the target audience. Often this stage is self-funded.

Start-up Stage - This is the stage where a new company gets off the ground. It has been determined that a market exists for your product. In this stage the direction of management takes shape.

First Stage - The production and marketing of your new product takes place now. Funds to get the new product out are needed.

Second Stage - During this period a new company usually does not show much profit, if any. Money is used for inventory and accounts receivable.

Third Stage - Funding during this stage is used to expand marketing efforts. Also working capital is needed. At this point sales are usually brisk and the company is turning a profit.

Fourth Stage - The company is now expanding to a medium sized business. Public stock offerings are being made to raise capital. This is also referred to as bridge financing. Financing is needed during the transition period until sufficient capital has been raised through the stock offering.

Acquisition Funding - During this phase companies grow by taking over other firms. Mergers very often occur at this point.

## FREE BUSINESS HELP FROM THE GOVERNMENT
The Federal Government offers free advice on business operating and financing through the Small Business Administration (SBA). I have listed a few of the publications that are designed to help small businesses. Call the SBA to get a list. Visit your local SBA online at http://SBA.gov or call the SBA at 1-800-8-ASK-SBA. The main office is located at:

1441 L Street NW.
Washington, DC. 20417

Management Assistance
(Order Form SBA-115A)
# 2.028 Business Plans for the Home Based Business

# 1.001 The ABC's of Borrowing
# 2.025 Thinking About Going into Business
# 1.004 Basic Budgets for Profit Planning
# 6.003 Incorporating a Small Business
# 1.016 Sound Cash Management
# 1.015 Budgeting a Small Business
# 2.027 How to Get Started with a Small Business Computer
# 4.019 Learning About Your Market
# 3.010 Techniques For Problem Solving
# 2.004 Problems In Managing a Family Owned Business
# 1.014 Getting the Facts For Income Tax Reporting
# 59.003 Loans for Small Businesses

The SBA also has set up a toll free answer desk to provide you with the latest information about their programs. The telephone number is 1-800-U-ASK-SBA.

The current menu categories are:
1. Starting Your Own Business
2. Financing Your Business
3. Counseling and Training
4. Local Services
5. Help for Minority Small Businesses
6. Veterans Affairs
7. Women Business Ownership
8. International Trade
9. Procurement and Government Contract Assistance

To encourage small business and private enterprise the government has set up a loan guarantee program. These loans and loan guarantees are available to those who don't qualify for traditional financing. To qualify for SBA funding you must have been turned down for a loan through a bank or other lending source.

The two basic types of loans are:

- SBA Loan Guarantees - The SBA will guarantee up to 90% of a loan made through a bank or other lending source. (This is the most common form of financial assistance through the SBA).

- SBA Direct Loans - Usually limited to $10,000-$15,000.

SBA loan guarantees are available up to $350,000 and can be financed usually up to 10 years.

Construction loans can be financed up to 20 years.

In order to qualify for a SBA loan you must first determine if your company is eligible. Companies eligible must have:
* Sales less than 10 million dollars gross per year (wholesale).
* Gross sales less than 2 million dollars per year (retail).
* Less than 250 employees (if a manufacturing business).
* Business must have net worth less than $2.5 million.
* Must be independently owned and not dominating its field.

When submitting a SBA loan application offer a complete business plan including financial projections, a resume outlining both personal and business skills and state whatever collateral you may have.

Check on the internet at http://www.sba.gov or consult your local telephone directory for the Small Business Administration Field Office near you.

Score
The Service Corps of Retired Executives (SCORE) is sponsored by the Small Business Administration (SBA). The SCORE staff is comprised of over 12,000 business executives who volunteer their time and expertise at over 800 locations throughout the United States, Puerto Rico and the US Virgin Islands. SCORE offers counseling and training to assist business owners and managers succeed. To contact the SCORE office nearest you contact 1-800-8-ASK-SBA.

Other Federal Assistance for Businesses
There are many different programs sponsored by the Federal Government to encourage business development. I have listed several programs below. As mentioned earlier, a complete list of publications is available from the Small Business Administration. The information contained therein is invaluable.

Business Loans and loan guarantees for low income business entrepreneurs.

Small Business Administration
Office of Business Loans
1441 L St. NW.
Washington, DC. 20416
http://www.sba.gov/

Business loans and loan guarantees and grants for investors with businesses In low-income areas.

Director of Economic Adjustment Division
Economic Development Association
Herbert Hoover Building
Washington, DC. 20230
http://www.eda.gov/

Business loans and loan guarantees for handicapped persons to start their own business.

Director
Small Business Administration
1441 L St. NW.
Washington, DC. 20416

http://www.sba.gov/

Business Loans and guarantees to business owners in towns with a population under 50,000.

Farmers Home Administration
US Department of Agriculture
Washington, DC. 20250
http://www.rurdev.usda.gov/

Grants, business Loans and loan guarantees for business owned by American Indians and Native Alaskans.

Director, Office of Indian Services
Bureau of Indian Affairs
18th & C Streets, NW.
Washington, DC. 20240
http://www.doi.gov/bureau-indian-affairs.html

Business loans and loan guarantees for investors and developers of rental apartment buildings.

Director, Office of Multifamily Housing Development
Department of Housing and Urban Development
Washington, DC. 20410
http://www.hud.gov/

Business loans and loan guarantees to small farmers.

Director
Farmers Home Administration
US Department of Agriculture
Washington, DC. 20250
http://www.rurdev.usda.gov/

Business loans and loan guarantees for starting businesses in a high unemployment area. The federal government will loan or guarantee up to $250,000 to start a business in high unemployment areas.

Director of High Unemployment Area Loans
Small Business Administration
1441 L St. NW.
Washington, DC. 20416
http://www.sba.gov/

## Minority Businesses

Various programs have been established to encourage the development of minority owned businesses. The Office of Minority Business Enterprise (OMBE) is within the Department of Commerce and works through local business development organizations in minority areas.
For a complete listing of available programs and locations in your area
Contact them at http://www.commerce.gov/ or http://www.commerce.gov/grants.html or their main office:

Office of Minority Business Enterprise
US Department of Commerce
14th Street and Constitution Avenue NW.
Washington, DC. 20230

Also contact:
Administrator for Minority Small Businesses
Small Business Administration
Room 602
1441 L Street NW.
Washington, DC. 20416

or online at http://www.sba.gov

Grants and Loans for Disadvantaged Businesses
The Office of Small and Disadvantaged Business Utilization (OSDBU) has many programs ranging from grants, loans, loan guarantees and technical assistance. Contact them at http://www.va.gov/OSDBU/ or the address below.

Office of the President
Office of Small and Disadvantaged Business Utilization
Washington, DC. 20250
http://osdbu.dot.gov/

# State Assistance for Businesses

Many years ago states began to recognize the importance of developing and maintaining business growth and development. Virtually every state has since established an agency that specifically handles business development. Assistance can range from planning and developing to tax breaks and other financial incentives. I have included the names of the state agencies set up to assist businesses.

State Business Centers
Alabama Planning and Industrial Development Board
> http://www.ecodevdirectory.com/alabama.htm

Arizona Small Business Development Board
> http://www.maricopa.edu/sbdc/stash.htm

Arkansas Industrial Development Board
> http://encyclopediaofarkansas.net/encyclopedia/entry-detail.aspx?entryID=42

California Department of Finance
> http://www.dof.ca.gov/

Connecticut Development Commission
> http://www.cslib.org/agencies/economicandcommunitydevelopment.htm

Delaware State Development Department
> http://dedo.delaware.gov/links.shtml

Florida Development Commission
> http://www.stateofflorida.com/development.html

Georgia Department of Industry and Trade
> http://www.georgia.org/

Hawaii Department of Planning and Economic Development
> http://hawaii.gov/dbedt/op/

Idaho Department of Commerce and Development
> http://www.idahoworks.com/

Illinois Board of Economic Development
> http://business.illinois.gov/assistance_edge.cfm

Indiana Department of Commerce
> http://www.in.gov/iedc/

Iowa Development Commission
> http://www.ecodevdirectory.com/iowa.htm

Kansas Department of Economic Development
http://www.kansascommerce.com/

Kentucky Department of Commerce
http://www.commerce.gov/Services/ssLINK/DEV01_005432

Louisiana Department of Commerce and Industry
http://www.lded.state.la.us/louisiana-businesses/business-resources.aspx

Maine Department of Economic Development
http://www.econdevmaine.com/

Maryland Department of Economic Development
http://www.choosemaryland.org/

Massachusetts Department of Commerce and Development
http://www.mass.gov/dep/cleanup/brownfie.htm

Michigan Department of Economic Development
http://www.michigan.gov/dleg

Minnesota Department of Business Development
http://www.mnsbdc.com/

Mississippi Development Authority
http://www.mississippi.org/

Missouri Chamber of Commerce and Industry
http://mochamber.com/

Montana Business Development
http://www.business.mt.gov/

Nebraska Department of Economic Development
http://www.neded.org/content/view/452/676/

Nevada Small Business Development Partners
http://www.nsbdc.org/who/partners/

New Hampshire Division of Economic Development
http://www.nheconomy.com/

New Jersey Division of Economic Development
http://www.njeda.com/
New York State Bureau of Department of Commerce
http://www.nysl.nysed.gov/ils/topics/business.htm

North Carolina Commerce and Industry Division
http://www.nccommerce.com/en/BusinessServices/

Ohio Development Department
http://www.odod.state.oh.us/

Oklahoma Department of Commerce and Industry
http://www.okcommerce.gov/

Oregon Department of Commerce
http://www.oregon.gov/DCBS/index.shtml

Pennsylvania Department of General Services
http://www.dgs.state.pa.us/

Rhode Island Chamber of Commerce
http://www.2chambers.com/rhode2.htm

South Carolina Economic Development Board
http://www.sciway.net/econ/boards.html

Tennessee Economic Development Council
http://www.tnedc.com/

Utah Industrial and Employment Planning
http://dced.utah.gov/

Vermont Development Department
http://www.thinkvermont.com/

Washington State Department of Commerce
http://www.cted.wa.gov/site/84/default.aspx

West Virginia Industrial Development Division
http://www.wvdo.org/contact.html

Wisconsin Department of Resource Development
http://commerce.wi.gov/BD/

Wyoming Business Council
http://www.wyomingbusiness.org/

## Local Assistance to Businesses

Nearly every city in the country has realized the important role businesses play in local economies. With so many businesses starting up each year local governments are scrambling to keep up. Business start-ups benefit everyone. It adds to tax dollars as well as jobs to the local economy and helps reduce the local welfare rolls. For the business owner it helps develop a strong sense of self worth. For these reasons local governments are working to attract new business by offering incentives as well as assistance. For a complete list of business assistance programs in your area consult your local business development agency usually located in your town, village or city clerk's office or city hall.

# Program Related Investments

Program related investments are funds made to advance a specific cause. These funds are made available usually by large corporations and foundations in the form of grants and loans.

Below are some of the major organizations that offer program related investments. Write to them and request information on program related grants and loans. This is just a small sample list. There are literally thousands of foundations in existence.

Ann Arbor Community Foundation
121 West Washington, Suite 400
Ann Arbor, MI. 48104

http://www.aaacf.org/grants.asp

Broyhill Foundation
Box 700
Lenoir, NC. 28633
http://www.tgci.com/funding/fdnresultnew.asp?thisID=4178

Cecil Charitable Trust
111 Broadway
New York, NY. 10006
http://www.cecillandtrust.org/

The Coca Cola Foundation
One Coca Cola Plaza
Atlanta, GA. 30313
http://www.thecoca-colacompany.com/citizenship/foundation_coke.html

The Collins Foundation
909 Terminal Sales Bldg.
Portland, OR. 97205

http://www.collinsfoundation.org/

Council for Aid to Education, Inc.
680 Fifth Ave
New York, NY. 10019

http://www.cae.org/

Coors Foundation
350 Clayton Street
Denver, CO. 80206

http://www.adolphcoors.org/

H & R Block Foundation
4410 Main Street
Kansas City, MO. 64111

http://www.hrblockfoundation.org/

Levi Strauss Foundation
1155 Battery Street
San Francisco, CA. 94106

http://www.levistrauss.com/citizenship/levistraussfoundation.aspx

Marathon Oil Foundation
539 S. Main Street
Findlay, OH. 45840
http://www.marathon.com/Social_Responsibility/Philanthropy/

The New Haven Foundation
One State Street
New Haven, CT. 06510
http://www.cfgnh.org/

Weingart Foundation
1200 Wilshire Blvd.
Los Angeles, CA. 90017
http://www.weingartfnd.org/

## Some Additional Programs

The National Endowment for the Arts
1100 Pennsylvania Ave, NW
Washington, DC. 20506
http://www.arts.endow.gov

Response and Recovery Directorate, Federal Emergency Management Agency,
Washington, DC 20472.
Telephone: (202) 646-3685.
Web Site Address: http://www.FEMA.gov

Rural Business-Cooperative Service
Department of Agriculture
Grant funds may be used to assist in the economic development of rural areas by providing technical assistance, training, and planning for business and economic development.

Range and Average of Financial Assistance: $2,000 to $500,000; $83,309.

Headquarters Office:         Rural Business-Cooperative Service, USDA, Specialty Lenders
Division, STOP 3225, Room 6767
1400 Independence Ave., SW.
Washington, DC 20250-1521.
Telephone: (202) 720-1400.
Web Site Address: http://www.rurdev.usda.gov

Office of Healthy Homes and Lead Hazard Control,
Department of Housing and Urban Development
Beneficiary Eligibility: Healthy Homes Initiative grants are intended to serve a broad array of beneficiaries including homeowners, rental property owners and public housing residents.

Range and Average of Financial Assistance: Healthy Homes Initiative grants awarded in FY 2000 ranged from $354,192 to $1,500,000.
Web Site Address: http://www.hud.gov/offices/lead

Bureau of Educational and Cultural Affairs, Department of State
Range and Average of Financial Assistance: Incentive grant $6,000; Mini-grant $2,000
http://exchanges.state.gov/education/rfgps/

NAFSA: Association of International Educators,
1307 New York Avenue, NW. Eighth Floor,
Washington, DC 20005-4701.
Telephone: (202) 737-3699. Fax: (202) 737-3657. E-mail:
Emil@nafsa.org
Web Site Address: http://nafsa.org

Department of Housing and Urban Development,
Office of Housing Assistance and Grant Administration
451 7th Street, SW.
Washington, DC 20410.
Telephone: (202) 708-3000.
Range and Average of Financial Assistance: Eligible tenants pay no more than 30 percent of their monthly-adjusted income for rent.
Web Site Address: http://www.hud.gov/fha/mfh/mfhsec8.html

Temporary Assistance for Needy Families
Range and Average of Financial Assistance: State Family Assistance Grants range from $21,781,446 to $3,733,817,784
Headquarters Office:
For all grants except Tribal grants:
Office of the Director,
Office of Family Assistance, Administration for Children and Families,
Department of Health and Human Services, 5th Floor, Aerospace Building
370 L'Enfant Promenade, SW.
Washington, DC 20447.

For Tribal Grants:

Office of the Director,    Office of Community Services, Administration for Children and Families,Department of Health and Human Services, 5th Floor, Aerospace Building, 370 L'Enfant Promenade, SW., Washington, DC 20447.

Web Site Address: Tribal TANF http://www.acf.dhhs.gov/programs/dts

Medical Assistance

Department of Health and Human Services

Headquarters Office:

Center for Medicaid and State Operations, Health Care

Financing Administration, Room C4-25-02, 7500 Security Boulevard

Baltimore, MD 21244.

Telephone: (410) 786-3870.

Web Site Address: http://www.hhs.gov

Public Housing Assistance

Beneficiary Eligibility: Low-income public housing residents.

Range and Average of Financial Assistance:

Headquarters Office:

Assistant Secretary for Public and Indian Housing Development,

Washington, DC 20410.

Telephone: (202) 708-0950.

Web Site Address: http://www.hud.gov/progdesc/pihindx.html

Minority Scholars Program

Beneficiary Eligibility: Funds awarded under this program are used to support full-time undergraduate students pursing a baccalaureate degree in an area of the food and agricultural sciences or a closely allied field.

Range and Average of Financial Assistance:

Awards ranged from $20,000 to $80,000 with the average award being $52,004.

Headquarters Office: Grant Programs Manager, Education Programs, CSREES,

Department of Agriculture, Room 3912, South Building,

Washington, DC 20250-2251.

Telephone: (202) 720-7854.

Web Site Address: http://www.reeusda.gov

Housing Application Packaging Grants

Beneficiary Eligibility: The targeted groups are very low- and low-income families without adequate housing in the colonials and designated counties.

Headquarters Office: Director, Single Family Housing Processing Division,

Rural Housing Service, Department of Agriculture

Washington, DC 20250

 Telephone:(202) 720-1474.

Web Site Address: http://www.rurdev.usda.gov

Food Stamps

Food and Nutrition Service,  Department of Agriculture

Range and Average of Financial Assistance: Varies by income and family size.

Headquarters Office: Deputy Administrator, Food Stamp Program, Food and Nutrition Service

Department of Agriculture, Alexandria, VA 22302.

Web Site Address: http://fns.usda.gov

Community Facilities Loans and Grants
Beneficiary Eligibility: Farmers, ranchers, rural residents, rural businesses, and other users of such public facilities in eligible applicant areas as set out above
Range and Average of Financial Assistance:
(Direct Loans) $50,000 to $2,500,000
(Guaranteed Loans) $100,000 to $2,500,000
(Grants) $10,000 to $100,000
Headquarters Office: Deputy Administrator, Community Programs, Rural Housing Service, Department of Agriculture
Washington, DC 20250- 3222.
Telephone: (202) 720-1490.
Web Site Address: http://www.rurdev.usda.gov

Minority Business Development Centers
Applicant Eligibility: There are no eligibility restrictions for this program. Applicants eligible to operate the Centers may include individuals, nonprofit organizations, for-profit firms, local and State governments, American Indian Tribes, and educational institutions.
Range and Average of Financial Assistance: $155,000 to $400,375.
Headquarters Office: Coordination Division
Minority Business Development Agency,
Department of Commerce
14th and Constitution Avenue, NW.
Washington, DC 20230.
Telephone: (202) 482-6022.
Web Site Address: http://www.mbda.gov

# Procurement Assistance to Small Businesses

Beneficiary Eligibility: Existing and potential small businesses will benefit.
Headquarters Office: Associate Administrator for Government Contracting
Small Business Administration
409 3rd Street, SW.
Washington, DC 20416.
Telephone:
(202) 205-6460.
Web Site Address: http://www.sba.gov
Business Development

OBJECTIVES:
To foster business ownership by individuals who are both socially and economically disadvantaged; and to promote the competitive viability of such firms by providing business development assistance including, but not limited to, management and technical assistance, access to capital and other forms of financial assistance, business training and counseling, and access to sole source and limited competition Federal contract opportunities, to help the firms to achieve competitive viability.

Beneficiary Eligibility: Socially and economically disadvantaged individuals and businesses owned and operated by such individuals; economically disadvantaged Indian tribes including Alaskan Native Corporations and economically disadvantaged Native Hawaiian organizations.

Headquarters Office: Associate Administrator for 8(a) Business Development,
Small Business Administration, 409 Third Street, SW., Washington, DC 20416.
Telephone:
(202) 205-6421.
Web Site Address: http://www.sba.gov

Job Opportunities for Low-Income Individuals
OBJECTIVES:
To promote the ability of welfare recipients and other low-income individuals and families to become financially self-sufficient by awarding grants to certain nonprofit organizations and community development corporations that will create new employment and business opportunities through: self-employment; micro-enterprise; new business ventures; expansion of existing businesses through technical and financial assistance; and non-traditional employment opportunities that will result in full-time permanent jobs for eligible participants.

Beneficiary Eligibility: Temporary Assistance for Needy Families (TANF) recipients and any low-income individuals, whose income does not exceed 100 percent of the official poverty guidelines.

Range and Average of Financial Assistance: The average is $500,000.
Division of Community Discretionary Programs
Office of Community Services, Administration for Children and Families
Department of Health and Human Services
370 L'Enfant Promenade, SW.
Washington, DC 20447
Telephone: (202) 401-5282.

Web Site Address: http://www.acf.dhhs.gov/programs/joli/welcome.htm
Supplemental Security Income
Beneficiary Eligibility: Individuals who have attained age 65 or are blind or disabled, who continue to meet the income and resources tests, citizenship/qualified alien status and U.S. residence requirements.

Eligibility may continue for beneficiaries who engage in substantial gainful activity despite disabling physical or mental impairments.

Headquarters Office: Office of Public Inquiries, Room 4100, Annex
Social Security Administration, Baltimore, MD 21235. Telephone: (410) 965-2736.
Web Site Address: http://www.ssa.gov

Micro loan Demonstration Program
OBJECTIVES:
To assist women, low-income, and minority entrepreneurs, business owners, and other individuals possessing the capability to operate successful business concerns and to assist small business concerns in those areas suffering from a lack of credit due to economic downturns.

Beneficiary Eligibility: Small businesses, minority entrepreneurs, nonprofit entities, business owners, women and low- income, and other individuals possessing the capability to operate successful business concerns.

Headquarters Office: Small Business Administration, Office of Financial Assistance, Microenterprise Development Branch
409 Third Street SW., Eighth Floor,
Washington, DC 20416. Mail Code 7881. Telephone: (202) 205-6490.
Web Site Address: http://www.sba.gov

Federal Supplemental Educational Opportunity Grants
Grants are for undergraduate study, and range from $100 to $4,000 per academic year. However, if reasonable study abroad costs exceed the cost of attendance at the home institution, the amount of the grant may exceed the $4,000 maximum by as much as $400.
Range and Average of Financial Assistance:

Regional or Local Office: Students should contact the educational institution(s) they attend or plan to attend. Educational institutions should contact the Regional Administrator for Student Financial Assistance in the appropriate ED Regional Office Headquarters Office:
Policy Development Division, Office of Student Financial Assistance
Department of Education
400 Maryland Avenue, SW.
Washington, DC 20202-5446.
Chief, Grants Branch.
Web Site Address: http://www.ed.gov/offices/OSFA

For additional federal programs check the Catalog of Federal Domestic Assistance
at your local library or online at http://www.cdfa.gov

Your satisfaction is guaranteed. However to protect against piracy of our products our return and refund policy is as follows:

Try our product for 30 days risk free. If you are dissatisfied with the Secret Book of Free Money results you could be entitled to a refund under specific circumstances:

* You must have actually tried to use the guide and be able to prove it.
* Send copies of letters from three separate sources rejecting your request.
* All must be sent within 30 days of receiving your book.

Mail all materials (copies of letters, request for refund, customer order number, etc.) to:

CM Consulting
Customer Service Department
P.O. Box 6311
St. Mary's, GA 31558

These are the only requirements. NO exceptions.

www.ingramcontent.com/pod-product-compliance
Lightning Source LLC
Chambersburg PA
CBHW081215170526
45165CB00009B/2834